Douglas Liversidge is a journalist and author of wide experience whose speciality is biography of prominent figures past and present. He spent many years in Fleet Street in various editorial capacities, spending some time as news editor of a national Sunday newspaper and as a writer for an international agency, publishing articles for newspapers and magazines in more than forty countries. During the war, he wrote anti Nazi commentaries for the BBC, and remains a keen observer of the contemporary scene. He is widely travelled and has journeyed to such remote regions as the Arctic and Antarctic. Douglas Liversidge has written two other highly successful royal biographies: *Queen Elizabeth II: The British Monarchy Today* and *Prince Charles: Monarch in the Making.*

Douglas Liversidge

Prince Philip
First Gentleman of the Realm

Panther

Published by Granada Publishing
in Panther Books 1977

ISBN 0 586 047670

Granada Publishing Limited
Frogmore, St Albans, Herts AL2 2NF
and
3 Upper James Street, London W1R 4BP
1221 Avenue of the Americas, New York, NY 10020 USA
117 York Street, Sydney, NSW 2000, Australia
100 Skyway Avenue, Toronto, Ontario, Canada M9W 3A6
Trio City, Coventry Street, Johannesburg 2001, South Africa
CML centre, Queen & Wyndham Streets, Auckland 1, New Zealand

First published in Great Britain by
Arthur Barker Ltd 1976
Copyright © Douglas Liversidge 1976

Made and printed in Great Britain by
Richard Clay (The Chaucer Press) Ltd
Bungay, Suffolk
Set in Linotype Times

The author and publishers are grateful to Hodder &
Stoughton Ltd for permission to publish the extract
in the second chapter from *Prince Philip: A Family
Portrait* by HM Queen Alexandra of Yugoslavia, the
rights of which are owned by Opera Mundi, of Paris.

Contents

List of Illustrations

THE MOUNTBATTENS

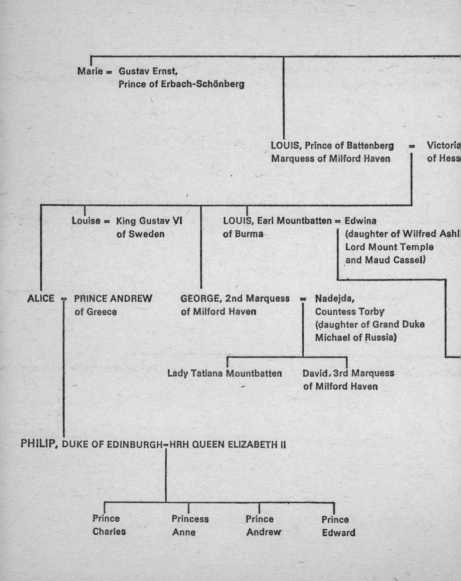

Marie = Gustav Ernst,
Prince of Erbach-Schönberg

LOUIS, Prince of Battenberg = Victoria
Marquess of Milford Haven   of Hesse

Louise = King Gustav VI   LOUIS, Earl Mountbatten = Edwina
of Sweden   of Burma   (daughter of Wilfred Ashl
                                                        Lord Mount Temple
                                                        and Maud Cassel)

ALICE = PRINCE ANDREW   GEORGE, 2nd Marquess = Nadejda,
of Greece   of Milford Haven   Countess Torby
                                                      (daughter of Grand Duke
                                                      Michael of Russia)

                              Lady Tatiana Mountbatten   David, 3rd Marquess
                                                          of Milford Haven

PHILIP, DUKE OF EDINBURGH = HRH QUEEN ELIZABETH II

Prince   Princess   Prince   Prince
Charles   Anne   Andrew   Edward

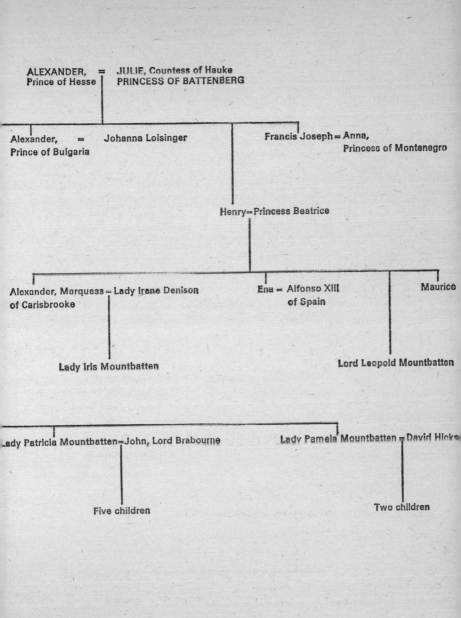

THE GREEK ROYAL FAMILY

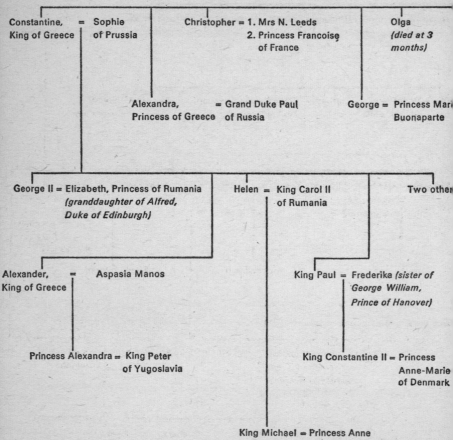

Constantine, = Sophie of Prussia

Christopher = 1. Mrs N. Leeds
2. Princess Francoise of France

Olga *(died at 3 months)*

Alexandra, Princess of Greece = Grand Duke Paul of Russia

George = Princess Mari Buonaparte

George II = Elizabeth, Princess of Rumania *(granddaughter of Alfred, Duke of Edinburgh)*

Helen = King Carol II of Rumania

Two other

Alexander, King of Greece = Aspasia Manos

King Paul = Frederika *(sister of George William, Prince of Hanover)*

Princess Alexandra = King Peter of Yugoslavia

King Constantine II = Princess Anne-Marie of Denmark

King Michael of Rumania = Princess Anne of Bourbon-Parma

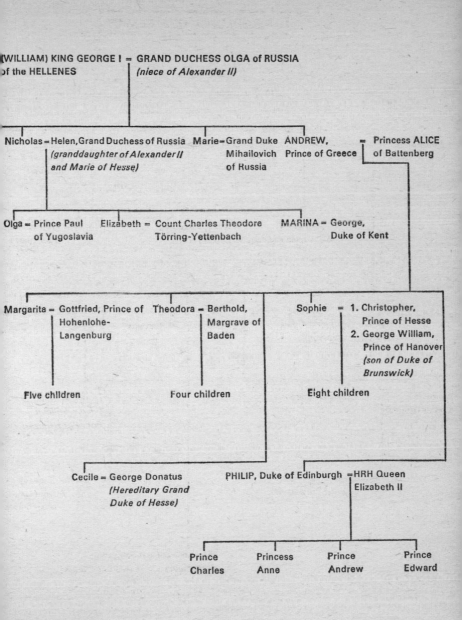

1

Greek Ancestry and Exile

It was feared that it would be a difficult birth. The strain of the unrelenting anxieties of late had been enfeebling. Not even the idyllic peace of Corfu could dispel the tension one had felt in nerve-torn Athens, so that when Princess Alice of Greece started her labour the Corfiot doctor, thinking that he might require something much more sturdy, had her carried from her bed down to the dining-room table. There, on 10 June 1921, by all accounts lying on a white embroidered table-cloth, she gave birth to her fifth child and only son: His Royal Highness Prince Philip of Greece. He would be a child of destiny.

The future Duke of Edinburgh was born at Mon Repos, a square Regency-style villa (for half a century the residence of British Commissioners) set on a promontory overlooking the sunlit expanse of the Ionian Sea. In summer the grounds, which fell away on the seaward side in a tumble of rocks, were ablaze with roses, and the warm air was heavy with the scent of orange, lemon, eucalyptus and other sweet-smelling trees. Ostensibly they were halcyon days. This Aegean pleasance had escaped the conflagration that for four years had devastated Europe, then flared afresh in the smouldering of war between Greece and Turkey. But drama lurked even in the year ahead; Prince Andrew of Greece, now commanding an army corps in Anatolia, would be in military disgrace and driven eventually with his family into exile, joining the royal flotsam swept by the merciless tides of revolution from the Courts of Europe.

But for the moment life was outwardly tranquil at Mon Repos, where the Princess's Scottish housekeeper, Mrs Agnes Blower, whose husband was the gardener and odd job man, supervised the domestics in this simple household. 'They did not live like Royals,' she revealed many years later, then living at an old people's home in Peterborough. Everything at the villa, she recalled, was inevitably primitive; there was no electricity, no gas, no running hot water – not even proper heating. 'We had a few untrained peasant girls to help, and two unwashed footmen who were rough fellows.' But when the Princess and her four young daughters wished to take a bath, water had to be heated in big pails in the kitchen on an old coal stove and then carried in buckets upstairs.

Devoted to the young Philip in this uncomplicated ménage was an English nanny, Miss Roose – 'Roosie' to the family – who had nursed Philip's cousins, the three daughters of Prince Nicholas of Greece: Marina, the future Duchess of Kent; Olga, the wife of Prince Paul of Yugoslavia; and Elizabeth, Countess Törring-Yettenbach. Like the formidable Mrs Blower, Roosie had faith solely in things British; weeks in advance of Philip's birth, her insistent demands for adequate supplies of English food and soap and Scottish woollens had been met by Lord Louis Mountbatten, Princess Alice's younger brother, in London.

In reminiscent mood, Mrs Blower recalled Philip as a plump and healthy infant with an impressive appetite. She also recalled that a problem cropped up when no clean cow milk was available on the length and breadth of Corfu; for the natives relied on the milk of goats. Thus when he was a little older she 'put a stop to his being fed on those messy foreign dishes which the Greek cook concocted', and instead she made for him 'nourishing rice and tapioca puddings and good wholesome Scots porridge'.

By princely standards Philip was born to unmistakable austerity. Shared with Roosie, the nursery room was unpretentious and sparsely furnished, and there was a noticeable paucity of toys. Not for Philip the companionship of a teddy bear. Sometimes Mrs Blower would sit with him 'on the old carpet and we played with red, white and blue bricks, roughly hewn from some old pieces of timber by a young gardener'. Philip lingered in her fading memory as 'a lively little lad' who, when he tired of building castles, ran around banging an empty tin with a stick. 'His favourite toy was his nanny's pin cushion. For hours he sat quietly in his cot, pulling the pins and needles out and pushing them in again. I always worried that he would hurt himself.' Even then, it seems, there were the incipient signs of Philip's later enthusiasm for anything mechanical. Some three months after Philip's birth, Princess Alice took her children to Britain for the funeral of her father, Admiral the Marquess of Milford Haven. In July 1922, there would be a second brief visit to England, this time for the wedding of her brother Louis to Edwina Ashley. And when he was two and a half years old Philip would embark on yet another journey to London – leaving the land of his birth for good.

Now that the lapse of time can define circumstances more clearly, it is apparent that politics, revolution and ancestry were the cardinal threads that wove the pattern of Prince Philip's life. On the paternal side he was born into that offshoot of the Schleswig-Holstein-Sonderburg-Glücksburg line that supplied kings to Greece. Like most European monarchies of this century, its throne would be unstable (a factor which would influence Prince Philip's life). There would be moments of high drama and in the end it would crash in the clash of political strife.

To understand the exile of Prince Andrew and his family (and its subsequent impact on his son's career), one must appreciate the historical circumstances which brought it about. The story of Prince Philip really begins on a day in 1863 when King Frederick VII of Denmark summoned to his study Prince William, his young grandson. The Greek throne was vacant, the royal youth was told, and he would be the next incumbent. Until that moment the tall, mischievous cadet from the Copenhagen naval school had contemplated a lifelong career in fighting ships, but now the astonished Willy – a mere stripling of seventeen and quite artless in the intricacies of statecraft – was plunged into the turbulence and chicaneries of Greek politics.

Greece felt the headiness of liberty after four centuries of servitude under the Ottoman Turks. From the struggle had emerged modern Greece, a pawn in the political rivalries of the

Protecting Powers – Britain, Russia and France. Added to this, the country festered with its unhealing feuds even among the resistance groups which had fought for freedom. Fortunately there was a smattering of realists. The revolutionary movement, the *Philike Hetairae*, which had fomented the 1821 rising, contended that Greece must seek a king 'so that all division and rivalry for preference should cease among us'. But the Courts of Europe offered no surfeit of candidates; the eruptive nature of Greek politics forewarned of uneasiness for the one who wore the crown. Prince Leopold of Saxe-Coburg, subsequently King of the Belgians, firmly declined it and the crown eventually came to rest on the head of Prince Otto, son of King Ludwig of Bavaria, an ardent Philhellene. The hapless Otto, well meaning but lacking insight into the Greek character, strove for thirty years to appease the inordinate demands of his mercurial people. One paramount aim he never achieved: to conquer the Turk with ruthless sword and regain the glories of the one-time Greater Greece. Nothing would ever satisfy the Greeks but the all-conquering march to Constantinople, their spiritual home. Otto reluctantly seized on the Crimean War to invade Epirus and Thesalay, but the Powers intervened and revolution in Greece was the strident aftermath. Otto hurriedly quit Athens to the disconcerting bark of musket shot, little realizing that he was merely the first royal exile to flee from Greece. In the years to come the Glücksburgs – among them Prince Philip himself – would be the victims of Greek aspirations and banished from Greece.

Meanwhile, in Athens the citizenry – to Russian and French annoyance – clamoured outside the British Embassy for another king. Brusquely they discarded the nominees of Russia and France and hopefully shouted for the appointment of Prince Alfred, Duke of Edinburgh, Queen Victoria's second son. Hellenic rejoicing, however, was ill-timed and premature; an adamant British monarch refused to let her son risk ignominy like the luckless Otto. Finally, only one name achieved mutual consent – the Queen's candidate, Prince William, the brother of the vivacious Alexandra, her future daughter-in-law. Because the Glücksburgs were distantly related to the Romanoffs, Willy was accepted by the Russians, and in France Napoleon III cunningly thought that he might exercise influence over a Dane. To the Greeks it seemed highly commendable, for the British had agreed to cede the Ionian Islands; on Corfu, Mon Repos would be another residence of the new Danish-born king.

Thus Prince Willy embarked from his native Denmark – with a conflicting sense of misgivings and optimism – and on the morning of 30 October 1863 the eighteen-year-old King George I (newly named after St George, the Greek national saint) received his first glimpse of his realm at Piraeus. As Otto's recently painted coaches crunched over the stony plain to his capital, Athens took shape before him. In the autumn air the Acropolis brooded high over the city, a gallimaufry of white tinged with gold by the sunlight. A spiteful wind bore the boom of the church bell on the bleak rock of Lykabettos and the thunder of gunfire on Acropolis Hill. And amid the cacophony of drums, trumpets and bugle blasts, punctuated by the sharp staccato of musketry, the swarthy Greeks ecstatically welcomed their young sovereign to the massive Austrian palace from which Otto had fled. This ran along one side of Kifissia Road, the domain of the well-to-do.

The Old Palace chilled the Danish heart. The draughty marble halls, which still bore traces of looting left by the mob, had little heating, and enamel stoves existed in only a few of the rooms. As time would tell, all attempts to make the palace more comfortable would be costly.

King George was crowned amid pungent incense and lengthy ritual the following day, and Horace Rumbold, the British chargé d'affaires, present as the King took his oath in the Athenian Assembly, wrote years later – '... he looked so young and artless that the experiment seemed to all of us questionable and indeed highly hazardous'. George I, who captivated with his charm, was vividly aware that he was alone among callous, unscrupulous politicians – 'many of whom had been steeped to the lips in treason', as Rumbold described them. With disarming candour, however, George, echoing the jocular words of Prince Leopold of the Belgians, impressed upon his Ministers that he always 'kept a portmanteau ready packed'; he would not hesitate to return to Denmark if the Greeks did not want him. Members of the dynasty he was to found would at times be starkly acquainted with those words.

Temporarily at least, King George coped with the political passions and intrigues of his subjects. In his first four years he never left Greece, travelling round his realm and mixing with all elements of his subjects. But it was a lonely life and he doubtless welcomed his councillors' suggestion that to guarantee the succession would have a steadying effect on both throne and people. Thus in 1867, to British consternation, King George accepted an invitation from the Tsar to spend nine months in Russia. This was the Russian move on the political chess-board to counter Queen Victoria, for the Tsarist regime was Turcophobe whereas Victoria and her Ministers were Turcophil. The object of this visit was twofold: to acquire a Russian wife and to learn how the Russians administered their empire.

St Petersburg still lay under its pall of snow when King George was received by Tsar Alexander II. George I was overwhelmed by the splendour and medieval pageantry of the Russian Court, which stressed the comparative drabness of his Hellenic environment. What princess, thought King George, could be tempted away from such magnificence? The answer came the day he visited the Tsar's brother, the Grand Duke Constantine, and his family at their country palace of Pavlovsk. At a ball given in his honour he noticed a girl observing him from behind the gallery curtains. 'Who is that fair girl with plaited hair?' he asked his partner, the Grand Duchess Vera. 'My sister Olga – still in the classroom,' she replied. 'She is not yet sixteen, so she never appears when we have guests.' Yet happily for King George, Olga arrived with the samovar at tea the next afternoon, curtsying shyly to the royal guest. To the astonishment of the Russian Court, the young King had, within weeks, successfully sought her hand in marriage. George and Olga were married in a splendid five-day ceremony at the chapel of the sumptuous Winter Palace and after a honeymoon at Ropcha embarked on the tedious journey to Greece. Years later their son Christopher would write: 'The bride was such a child that she brought a whole family of dolls with her to her new country. For the entry into Athens she wore a little dress in the Greek colours of blue and white, and the crowds in the streets shouted themselves hoarse in welcome. Her shy youth and beauty conquered their impressionable hearts that day and, through all the vicissitudes of our house, she at least never lost their love.'

From that union – the paternal grandparents of Prince Philip – sprang the Royal House of Greece. When a son was born to Queen Olga the following year, he was christened Constantine by popular demand, in memory of the last Emperor of Byzantine Greece. Jubilant crowds visualized in the boy-prince the link with an impressive past and a portent of a glorious future. A royal son had been born on sacred soil and Greeks – even in the remoter parts – entertained the mystical belief that the destiny of a proud race would be achieved. This would be the bugbear that would haunt King George I and his descendants. Meanwhile the great white palace gradually shed its loneliness and its gaunt walls rang with the young voices of a native-born family: Constantine, George, Nicholas, Andrew (destined to be Prince Philip's father) and Alexandra and Marie. Another daughter, Olga, born in 1881, died the same year. Only King George would adhere to his Protestant faith; the Queen chose for her children – and later her grandchildren, including Prince Philip – the Greek Orthodox Church.

By royal standards life at the Old Palace was spartan. In manhood during exile, Prince Christopher would recall: 'There was only one bathroom in the whole place, and no one had ever been known to take a bath in it, for the simple reason that the taps would scarcely ever run and, on the rare occasions when they could be coaxed into doing so, emitted a thin trickle of water in which the corpses of defunct roaches and other strange animals floated dismally ... The cold of the Palace was almost unbearable. The wind whistled down the corridors and curled like a lash in and out of the lofty salons.' For heating, the family relied on antique stoves and the lighting came from oil lamps which smelt and smoked. Even so there was merriment. In the voluminous ballroom there was cycling and roller-skating, in which the King sometimes took part. 'My father, although he was habitually strict enough to keep us all in awe of him, was the best of playfellows and could generally be persuaded to lead the procession, winding in and out among the pillars, and after him would come the whole family in order of seniority – I bringing up the rear. We would start off in stately fashion until, often as not, we smashed into one another and came to earth in a tangled heap, some of us shrieking with laughter, others with the pain of bruises.'

It was to escape the austerity of the palace that the King bought in 1871 an estate of pine woods and heather-clad hills at Tatoi at the foot of Mount Parnes. Built in the English Elizabethan style, the mansion gazed on forest slopes across the Attic plain to the Saronic Gulf. Here, away from the stridence of Greek politics, the family could live in peace, roaming over its many acres – the domain of stag, boar and wolf – or ride in yellow Viennese carriages along the many miles of highways cut through the pines. Years later Prince Andrew would regale his son Philip with those times, highlighting the celebrations on the King's and the Queen's birthdays – events which were as eagerly anticipated by the royal children as by the peasantry. In the darkness, torches cast their fiery glow and the people danced to the music of fiddles and concertinas, pipes and drums; and from his children's hands the King took golden coins, pressing one to the forehead of each perspiring player. The carcases of sheep sizzled on the spits and the peasants drank Deceleia, the wine made by the King from his Tatoi vineyards.

George I was happy when mingling with his subjects, treating equally all grades of society (an egalitarian characteristic that would be reflected in his grandson Philip). Hence his dynastic motto: 'My strength is in the love of my people.' But it was not the peasants, the humbler folk, but the politicians who dictated affairs in Greece. The hatreds and vendettas and the raucous clamour for the Greater Greece meant tolerating at times indignities and humiliations. Sometimes the King would say: 'I feel as though I am living on the top of a volcano.' On occasions the bags would be packed, with the Royal

Family ready to quit Greece in a British warship waiting at Piraeus. But uncompromising exile never became reality until later reigns. In the meantime, Glücksburg destinies were entwined through marriage with those of other noted European families. Some had already reached their zenith of power, to be snuffed out by the whirlwind of war and revolution. Others would survive, and an admixture of disaster and success would be the ancestral alchemy moulding the fortunes of a boy yet to be born – Prince Philip of Greece.

In 1889 Constantine, the Diadoch or Crown Prince, married Princess Sophie Dorothea of Hohenzollern, the granddaughter of Queen Victoria and sister of Kaiser Wilhelm, a connection that would have serious repercussions on the Glücksburgs in the First World War. In the same year Alexandra, the King's eldest daughter, married the Grand Duke Paul of Russia. Thirteen years elapsed before Nicholas took the Grand Duchess Helen of Russia as his bride (one day one of their daughters would be known as Marina, Duchess of Kent). Next, Prince Andrew married Princess Alice of Battenberg in 1903, and five years later his brother George was joined in matrimony with Princess Marie Bonaparte, a descendant of Lucien, Napoleon's brother. In 1920 Prince Christopher married a rich American, Mrs Nancy Leeds, and after her death he married again – this time Princess Françoise of France, sister of the Count of Paris. Like her sister, King George's second daughter also took a Russian spouse – the Grand Duke Mihailovich.

It was the wedding of Prince Andrew and Princess Alice which is significant to this book. Both had been guests at the coronation of Britain's King Edward VII in 1902. Alice, who had served Queen Alexandra as a maid-of-honour, was seventeen and Andrew, an officer in the Greek Army, was twenty. But they had also met at Darmstadt where stood the ancestral home of the Grand Dukes of Hesse and by Rhine; as part of his training, Andrew had been attached to the Hessian 23rd Dragoon Guards.

His army career had been planned in childhood. King George had endured the rigours of a naval cadetship and did not believe in pampering his offspring. Maybe Constantine, the first-born, suffered the most arduous discipline of all but the regimen set for Andrew was quite exacting. There was the detested cold bath at six each morning and a simple breakfast. The first lessons lasted from seven until nine and after a visit to the martinet father they were resumed, followed by a leavening of physical exercises and gymnastics conducted by German instructors. A welcome interval was a chat with his mother in her drawing-room before continuing his studies. At 7.30 p.m. he retired to bed.

Even in childhood Prince Andrew revealed a quick intellect and independent mind, traits which today are manifest in his son. The question of language was a case in point. In his memoirs, Prince Christopher describes how the Greek Court – more so when there were visits from foreign relatives – was a Tower of Babel: 'My parents spoke German to one another and English to us children, except to my brother Andrew, who flatly refused to speak anything but Greek; we spoke Greek in the nursery and schoolroom.'

At fourteen Prince Andrew's training became perhaps even more rigid, when he joined the Athens military school and was drilled by German officers. Three years later the routine was intensified on beginning his commissioning course. The choice of private tutor was the Greek Major Panayotis Danglis. Noted in the world of ballistics he created a remarkable mountain gun which, attached to the back of a mule, could be assembled in ninety seconds, a conspicuous advance on the antiquated weaponry which the Greeks hauled by means of men and bullocks over back-breaking country. The day would come when the seemingly pro-royalist Danglis would treacherously attack the monarchy. But for the moment he collaborated in the King's inflexible programme for his son, recording that the tall, handsome prince was quick and intelligent. It has been claimed that at the outset Prince Andrew tended to be indolent but the formidable curriculum prepared for him left scant scope for idleness: fortifications and artillery, military history, technology, geography and topography. Other tutors for more formal educational subjects jostled for Andrew's limited time.

It was a stern programme which lasted for eighteen months and allowed no respite. In that time Danglis followed the Prince like some inescapable shadow – even when in the spring of 1900 the Royal Family relaxed at Mon Repos. Neither was Andrew permitted to discard Danglis and his textbooks when in the summer of that year he visited Crete where his brother, Prince George, had been installed by the Protecting Powers as High Commissioner.

With that same tenacity and industry which is now displayed by Prince Philip, Prince Andrew reaped his reward in the end. On 14 May 1901, the Prince began three days of examinations which earned him the plaudits of an unnerving board: King George, the Crown Prince Constantine, Prince Nicholas, the Archbishop, the Prime Minister, the Minister of War, the Commandant of the Athens Military Academy, the King's military ADC, and the bevy of tutors. On the final day the King proudly gave a toast to his son and commissioned him a subaltern in the cavalry. To Danglis went the Gold Cross of the Order of the Redeemer.

King George had been demanding in Prince Andrew's upbringing. Now he was equally liberal in encouraging his son's courtship. Princess Alice had been born at Windsor Castle, in the same bed in which her own mother, Princess Victoria of Hesse (a granddaughter of the Queen-Empress and grandmother of Prince Philip) had also been born. It has been implied that the narrow world of Victorian punctiliousness and Darmstadt provincialism which Alice inhabited – a world made even narrower by the acute deafness which had afflicted her since infancy – all the more endeared to her the lively cavalry officer who sported a monocle. There is evidence, however, that although the Prince had genuinely won her heart, her family at first were lukewarm to the union. They admired the young practical joker with the humorous turn of phrase, but by the rigid standards of the social hierarchy then in Europe he was impecunious. That was not all. In her memoirs, Prince Philip's cousin, Princess Alexandra, the former Queen of Yugoslavia, has revealed that the 'doting great-uncle, King Edward VII, running his hand through Alice's soft ringlets, declared bluffly that no throne in Europe was too good for her', adding that 'it may be that the King raised an eye-brow at an unpromising match to a younger son – indeed, the youngest but one – of the comparatively new Royal House of the Hellenes'. Moreover, it was imperative under the Royal Marriage Act to secure the King's consent to the marriage. In due course this was forthcoming, but the King stipulated that the bride should marry according to Protestant rites.

The engagement was officially announced on 5 May 1903 and received the seal of royal approval the following night. At a dinner party given at Marlborough House by the Prince and Princess of Wales (the future King George v and Queen Mary), King Edward and Queen Alexandra and members of the Battenberg, Greek and Danish families drank toasts to the betrothed. Britain learnt from the *Daily Express* how the match 'originally met with strong opposition from the bride's relatives owing to the bride's and bridegroom's lack of money, but Prince Andrew wooed his love boldly and would not be discouraged'. The romance had survived; although years later, during Philip's childhood, it would founder. 'Love triumphed at last over considerations of prudence, and it is stated that several imperial and royal relatives have between them generously contributed sufficient funds to enable the young couple to start life without excessive financial sorrows. A wedding present from the Tsar of £100,000 was the largest contribution.' The British Byron Society, linked with the English milord who had vehemently campaigned to free Greece, announced the forging of a further bond of union between Albion and Hellas. Characteristically, the Greeks marked the event by igniting dynamite at the Sultan's palace in Salonika.

Though English by inclination, the bride's father, Admiral Prince Louis of Battenberg, Director of Naval Intelligence at the British Admiralty, decided on Darmstadt, the ancestral home, as the setting for his daughter's wedding. The guest list graphically illustrated how interlaced were the Battenbergs with Europe's reigning houses. Queen Alexandra, accompanied by the Princesses Victoria and Beatrice, represented King Edward vii. The Tsar Nicholas and his family arrived with customary pomp, bringing also the Imperial Russian Choir to sing lusty national songs and Gregorian chants. The Russian contingent also included the Grand Duke Paul. The bridegroom's parents, King George and Queen Olga of Greece, attended with their sons and daughters-in-law, and among the galaxy of guests were the Kaiser's brother, Prince Henry of Prussia, and most of the minor royalty from all over Germany. Austrian archdukes and Danish and French princes came with their suites, and the Battenberg party included a nanny with a boy of three, who came to be known as Earl Mountbatten of Burma. Many would be consumed in the holocaust of war and revolution, but for the present they lived in a secure and carefree world. To ease the strain of hospitality imposed on his brother-in-law, the Grand Duke Ernest, Prince Louis accommodated some of the guests at Heiligenberg Castle which his father, Prince Alexander of Hesse, had bequeathed to him.

The ceremonial was three-fold: a civil ceremony to meet German laws; a Protestant wedding to satisfy the British sovereign; and, finally, the impressive rites of the Greek Orthodox Church. As Andrew's brothers, Nicholas and Christopher, held the golden crowns over the heads of the bride and bridegroom in this spectacular climax, there was an embarrassing moment due to Princess Alice's deafness. Confused by the Archpriest's capacious beard, she failed to read his lips. When questioned if she was willing to take the bridegroom as a husband, she answered 'No'. Asked if she had promised to wed someone else, she replied 'Yes'. It required a sharp nudge from Christopher to put matters right.

The rituals ended, formality was cast aside. At dinner in the huge baroque dining-hall in Darmstadt's Old Palace, the suites were dispensed with. Later, even the scarlet-liveried servants were excused, the Grand Duke and Prince Andrew's brothers serving as waiters. Admiral Mark Kerr, Prince Louis's biographer, himself a guest, described how 'everyone was skylarking about, more like a Bank Holiday on Hampstead Heath than a royal ceremonial'. He further recounts a contretemps involving the unpredictable Grand Duchess Vera (with whom King George I had danced at Pavlovsk): 'I was given the bridegroom's overcoat and hat to hold, and was standing next to the Grand Duchess Vera when Prince George of Greece seized the hat and put it on his aunt's head, knocking her spectacles off and damaging her coiffure. She was, I think, one of the first ladies with bobbed hair I had ever seen. Deprived of her spectacles she could not see who was the aggressor. However, she pulled the hat off and started to hit me over the head with it. Queen Alexandra, who was standing close behind and saw the whole incident, found the opportunity for having a little joke, so she went back until she found my sister, and told her, "Your brother has been so funny. He has put his hat on the Grand Duchess Vera's head, and knocked her spectacles off." My sister evidently thought the champagne had been too much for me, and hurried forward to reprove and, if necessary, remove me.' Of the couple's departure, he wrote:

'Showers of rice and slippers followed them as they drove out under a strong electric light, near which was gathered a group of German detectives with ammunition boots on their feet and umbrellas in their hands. The carriage had to go about sixty yards and then turn into a street which was lined with spectators about six deep, waiting to see the departure of the bride and bridegroom. Almost directly they had started the Emperor of Russia called out, "Come along, we can catch them again outside," and started to run. Everyone in their tiaras, ribbons and stars followed him, the children of the party hanging on to his coat-tails. As they came out under the light, it appeared to the detectives that something unusual was happening, for the paper bags must have looked like bombs, and the satin shoes gleaming under the searchlight appeared very like daggers. Thereupon they shouldered their umbrellas and joined the rush. The Emperor went straight for the backs of the people ... Putting his head down, he rammed them and gradually pushed his way through ... and reached the street ... when Princess Alice [was] bowing her acknowledgements to the cheering crowd. At this moment she received the contents of the full bag of rice, which the Emperor had carried, in her face, followed by the satin shoe. Casting dignity aside, she caught the shoe, and leaning over the back of the carriage hit the Emperor on the head with it, at the same time telling him exactly what she thought of him.'

For the most part, married life meant living in the cheerless Old Palace in Athens, but Prince Andrew and Princess Alice could relax at Tatoi where the King had built houses for members of his family. Prince Philip's eldest sister, Margarita, was born in 1905, and Theodora arrived in the following year. Cecile came into the world in 1911, and Sophie three years later. While Prince Andrew pursued his military career, Princess Alice attended the School of Greek Embroidery, studying the intricacies of this national folk-craft. In time she would qualify to assist the school's founder, Lady Egerton, wife of the British ambassador, and instruct the students herself. Unaware of it then, Princess Alice – flaxen-haired, profoundly religious and of an extremely sober mind – would commercialize her hobby for other refugees in exile. Holidays at Corfu and visits to relatives abroad – notably to her father's London home in Spring Gardens near Admiralty Arch – punctuated this unflurried routine.

Yet one never quite knew when political smouldering would erupt. George I had now to contend with the Military League led by revolutionary-minded men like General Pangalos and Colonel Plastiras. The King, subjected to a gradual erosion of powers, saw in his Prime Minister Eleutherios Venizelos the spectre of republicanism growing nearer. In 1909 the League compelled Prince Andrew and his brothers to resign their commissions in both army and navy, yet such was the fickle state of the Greeks that three years later the nation was temporarily united. Another war was imminent; Serbia, Bulgaria and Montenegro had signed a military pact against the hated Turk. Ostensibly Greece remained outside the treaty, yet from the balcony at the Old Palace in September 1912 King George, with Prince Andrew standing beside him holding a candle, read the order for general mobilization. The street lights in Kifissia Square picked out the milling crowd below. The discordance of tram bells, motor horns, bugles and tin cans signified the people's approval.

By the time Montenegro declared war on Turkey on 8 October, the Greek Army, commanded by Crown Prince Constantine, had assembled at Larissa. This time they fell on the Turks with such ferocity that by 9 November the Greeks stood looking down on Salonika. Officers shared privations with the men. We read, for instance, of Constantine and his headquarters staff, which included Prince Nicholas and Prince Philip's father, sheltering in a mountain church hungry and sodden. Lacking baggage they rested on straw and in the altar candle-light ate with bare hands a young roasted pig. Constantine, accompanied by Nicholas and Andrew, rode into Salonika on 10 November at the head of his army. A tremendous downpour greeted King George (accompanied by Princess Alice who had brought much needed medical supplies) as he entered Salonika the next day. He would never see Athens again. While walking unguarded among the people, he was shot dead in the street by a Macedonian Greek. The motive would never be known.

Constantine acceded to a shaky throne, to a rising crisis which culminated the day after Prince Philip's fourth sister was born. Fatal shots were fired at Sarajevo, resulting in the bloodbath of the First World War. Inevitably members of the Greek Royal Family were torn by individual loyalties, a conflict of allegiances which would be repeated and witnessed by Prince Philip himself when Europe was again set aflame in 1939. King Constantine professed neutrality yet no one could ignore the fact that his consort was the Kaiser's sister.

In contrast, Prime Minister Venizelos, firm in his demands to join the Western Allies, resigned to found his revolutionary committee at Salonika. Athens festered with espionage and the secret police and daylight exposed the battered corpses of rival factions in the streets. Rumour was rife. At Tatoi the King and Queen almost lost their lives in a forest fire, reputed to be the nefarious plot of Allied agents, whilst Constantine was alleged to be radioing reports to the enemy with equipment secreted among the trees. And although it had been constructed in 1894, the King was even accused of building a landing-stage at Mon Repos so that German U-boats could refuel.

In desperation, during July 1916, Constantine despatched his brothers Nicholas and Andrew to the Allied countries to explain the truth. Neither Prince Andrew nor Princess Alice, whose father and two brothers were in the Royal Navy, held German sympathies. Yet in Britain Prince Andrew came under virulent attack, the *Daily Mail* in particular fomenting this campaign of hate. In an article entitled 'How Prince Andrew of Greece Repays Our Hospitality', this newspaper published a photograph portraying the Prince accompanied by Colonel Metaxas. The article claimed that 'Prince Andrew has been scheming with Colonel Metaxas, formerly of the Greek general staff and a prominent member of the Germanophile group, who had smuggled out information from Greece to Berlin, disclosing Allied troop movements'. Moreover, 'proof that the Greek princes have been intriguing behind the Allies' back is provided by letters intercepted by the British Secret Service'. Prince George, Andrew's brother, was alleged to have been 'the leader of pro-German irregulars and the organizer of ambushes against Allied troops'. Prince Andrew was deeply embroiled. London newspapers claimed that he had intrigued with Constantine's Prime Minister Gounaris and Colonel Metaxas, as well as the former German ambassador in Athens, Count Mirbach, and the Kaiser's emissary Baron von Schenk, who 'had paid substantial sums of money to stir up trouble against the Allies in Greece'. With the nauseating memory of newspaper placards denouncing 'Tino's Treachery', Prince Andrew returned to Greece from his hopeless mission. The final humiliation was the Allied bombardment of Athens.

King Constantine, with other members of his family – including Prince Philip's parents – found uneasy sanctuary in Switzerland. Of those anxious days, Prince Christopher recorded:

'We lived in Switzerland for the next three years, spending our summers in Zurich and Lucerne, and our winters at St Moritz. It was ... a hand-to-mouth existence with its daily worries over our ways and means. Our private incomes

were stopped and we had to depend on borrowed money ...
Just when we were wondering where in the world the next
quarter's rent was coming from, someone always stepped
into the breach ... As political exiles we were regarded as
dangerous and suspicious characters and our friends could
only visit us in the strictest secrecy, for we were subject to a
rigid espionage and had all our correspondence censored.'

Constantine's son Alexander had been left on the throne
but the young King was a mere puppet manipulated by the
Venizelos clique. His humiliation ceased dramatically in 1920.
While calling at the house of his vineyard keeper at Tatoi, the
King was fatally bitten by one of two pet monkeys which
attacked his Alsatian dog. Years later Winston Churchill would
write: 'A quarter of a million persons died of this monkey's
bite.' Actually the impact would be greater. Venizelos, who
was already at war with the Turks in Anatolia, now wrongly
thought the time to be opportune for proclaiming a republic.
Unpredictably, however – to the chagrin of Britain and France
– the majority of the people voted in a plebiscite for the recall
of ex-King Constantine.

History takes many unexpected twists and it is ironical that,
but for British hostility to King Constantine – and consequently
to his brothers – Prince Philip would not have become the
'First Gentleman of the Realm' in Britain today. Whitehall
and the Quai d'Orsay united in informing the Greeks that 'the
restoration of a King whose disloyal attitude during the War
had caused grave embarrassment must be regarded as ratifica-
tion by Greece of his hostile attitude'. Venizelos had expedited
economic disaster in Greece. His mad obsession to regain the
Greater Greece and secure Hellenic republicanism had blinded
him to harsh reality. This, unfortunately, was Constantine's
inheritance and without Anglo-French political power and
financial aid nothing could rescue Greece from catastrophe.
He was faced with a dilemma: national pride had to be satisfied and to withdraw from Asia Minor would expose the Greek
nationals there to massacre and fire. Inevitably the war must
continue. The situation was not without anxieties for Prince

Andrew. To raise the troops' morale, it was felt imperative that a member of the Royal Family should take command of an army corps in the field. The choice fell to the reluctant Prince.

Soon after Prince Philip's birth, his father left for the front. Prince Andrew would later protest that the modern equipment which Danglis, his one-time tutor, had invented was never forthcoming. In August 1922 the world's press announced Greek defeat by Mustapha Kemel, the founder of new Turkey. Rout and panic followed retreat. Thousands of Greeks were massacred at Smyrna, burnt or drowned in an orgy of death. Tragically for Prince Andrew his troops had been the first to collapse. Under the onslaught of revolution led by Plastiras and Pangalos, Constantine quit the throne in favour of his son George, who would be the pawn of military dictators until Greece accepted republicanism on 1 May 1923.

Contemptuous of incompetence (a trait which is also discernible in Prince Philip) Prince Andrew had asked to be relieved of his command on 22 July 1922. By October he had returned to his family at Mon Repos. His intolerance of the stupidities and intrigues of the politicians and general staff was reflected in his letter to General Papulas, the commander-in-chief, dated 22 July 1921. Commenting on the brigade of mountain artillery which only arrived after his many requests, he wrote:

'Its personnel was so ignorant that for days it was unable even to find the Division, in spite of all my instructions. It was so untrained that in yesterday's action at Alpanos, in which the Division fought for six hours against a strongly entrenched force of 8,000 men, only four guns of one battery supported the attack. The brigade, during the whole of the action, was engaged in making endless reconnaissances, and when it did fire once, it fired at our own troops.'

The revolutionaries had assured him that there would be no interference with his life at Corfu, but in October 1922 he was summoned to a court of the revolutionary committee in Athens.

Taken by destroyer to the mainland he was required, he was told, as a witness in the action against the 'royal traitors'. But instead he was confined to prison and indicted of high treason. In addition to himself, three ex-prime ministers, a number of ministers and military officers were accused of the calamitous results of the war.

After the first trial on 13 November, Demetrios Gounaris and five others died before firing squads. The trial of Prince Andrew and five generals was convened for 2 December and, philosophically, Prince Philip's father awaited death. Execution might have been the tragic outcome but for the courage of Princess Alice. Leaving her children in Corfu, she hastened to Athens, frantically appealing to her brothers in London, the Pope and King Alfonso of Spain (her cousin Ena's husband), to intervene. Lord Louis Mountbatten talked with King George v, Prince Andrew's cousin; he then approached Bonar Law, the Prime Minister. Unfortunately Lord Curzon, the Foreign Secretary, was attending the League of Nations in Geneva, thus causing a delay in what was rapidly becoming a somewhat incongruous state of affairs. For so long the 'German Greeks' had been the butt of Britain's bitter condemnation, but now a Foreign Office telegram to Athens disclosed: 'The King is most anxious concerning Prince Andrew. Please report on His Royal Highness's present position, and continue to keep us informed by telegraph of any developments.'

Prince Christopher, Andrew's younger brother, who was married to an American heiress and no longer resided in Greece, was also anxious. Returning to Athens he made overtures, which proved abortive, to save his brother's life.

'No one was allowed to go near Andrew except his valet [he wrote later]. Guards kept strictest watch and confiscated all letters and parcels. Finally I hit on the expedient of writing a letter on cigarette paper, rolling it tightly and putting it with cigarettes into his valet's case. Andrew answered it with a short note, full of courage, but ... I knew that he had no longer any hope of regaining his freedom. He had just had a conversation with a former school-fellow, Pangalos, now

Minister of War and instigator of his trial, that left him small grounds for optimism. Plastiras, incidentally, had served under Prince Andrew in the disastrous campaign.

"How many children have you?" Pangalos had asked suddenly, and when my brother told him, he shook his head: "Poor things, what a pity, they will soon be orphans!"'

But Curzon acted. Serving in Britain's foreign service at that time was Commander Gerald Talbot, formerly the naval attaché in Athens. Curzon instructed him to get Prince Andrew and his family out of Greece. Travelling with false papers he arrived in the Greek capital on 28 November, a few days before the trial. It is said that if necessary Talbot had planned to abduct the Prince, but after a lengthy talk with Pangalos, in the early hours of 30 November, the British Legation in Athens telegraphed to the Foreign Office in London:

'... Mr Talbot has obtained this evening a promise from Minister of War and also from Colonel Plastiras, the two leaders of government, that Prince Andrew will not be executed but allowed to leave the country in charge of Mr Talbot. Following is the arrangement agreed upon:

'Prince will be tried on Saturday and sentenced to penal servitude or possibly to death. Plastiras will then grant pardon and hand him over to Mr Talbot for immediate removal with Princess by British warship to Brindisi or to any other port en route to England. British warship must be at Phaleron by midday December 3rd and captain should report immediately to legation for orders, but in view of necessity for utmost secrecy, captain should be given no indication of reason for voyage.

'This promise has been obtained with greatest difficulty and Talbot is convinced that above arrangement be strictly adhered to so as to save Prince's life. As success of plan depends on absolute secrecy of existence of this arrangement, even Prince and Princess cannot be given hint of coming. Talbot is convinced that he can rely on word given him and I see no other possibility of saving Prince's life.'

Actually the sentence on the Prince was imprisonment, deprivation of rank and titles and banishment for life, but the wording of the pardon was harsh and would inscribe itself indelibly on Prince Andrew's mind. He was found guilty of the ignominy of disobeying orders and abandoning his post. 'But consideration being given to extenuating circumstances of lack of experience in commanding a large unit, he has been degraded and condemned to perpetual banishment.' (Many years later, when documents of British foreign policy from 1919 to 1939 were due to be published, this and an earlier telegram announcing Talbot's efforts to rescue the royal prisoner were submitted to Sir Michael Adeane, then Queen Elizabeth's Private Secretary, for fear there might be some 'objection to their being printed'. Prince Philip merely objected to an editor's footnote relating to the verdict. In a short message, he recommended its deletion: 'People might think it was true.')

The rest of the accused were shot. During the night Pangalos visited the prison and drove the Prince and Talbot to the cruiser *Calypso* where Princess Alice was waiting. At Corfu the four daughters, and Prince Philip in Roosie's arms, were taken on board. Years would elapse before the infant Philip would appreciate the drama of the recent weeks and the significance of exile. On the voyage to Brindisi sailors lined an orange box as a cot – in a sense his baptism into the Royal Navy. In Rome his parents had an audience with the Pope, Prince and Princess Andrew thanking His Holiness for exercising influence at the trial. Then the family continued to London where Talbot, who had preceded them, was surprised to be knighted by the King.

2

The Early Influences

Now safe in London, Prince Andrew and his family stayed
temporarily at Kensington Palace in the grace-and-favour
apartment of Princess Alice's mother, the Dowager Marchioness
of Milford Haven. The baby Philip, fair and blue-eyed, was
the centre of attraction at family reunions. In the passage of
time, the most significant of all the relatives in the child's life
would be the Mountbatten uncles: George, the brilliant second
Marquess of Milford Haven (whose wife, the daughter of the
Grand Duke Michael of Russia, had been ruthlessly deprived of
her wealth by the Bolsheviks) and his younger brother, Lord
Louis, a man of action and creative flair with an uncanny ability
to simplify complex problems. Both would loom large in moulding the child's unique destiny, and even now the precise pattern was being formulated for the future. For a while Philip
would be separated from his parents (a prelude to lengthy
separations in later childhood) who, in the New Year, travelled
to New York to visit Prince and Princess Christopher, the widow
of the American millionaire William B. Leeds, before cruising in their yacht from Canada to Palm Beach.

After the mind-scarring effect of Greek politics, it was no more
than a remedial interlude; Prince Andrew could not escape from
certain inexorable problems. First there was the question of lost
nationality. This, however, presented no permanent obstacle,
for his cousin King Christian x of Denmark now issued the
Prince and his family with Danish passports. Thus, although
Prince Philip was born on Greek soil, in effect he quickly re-
verted to the nationality of his ancestral origin. More paramount and persistent in his father's mind was the urgent task
of maintaining his family. True or not, it is on record that King

George V, with typical bluffness, had pronounced that he would 'not pay for any extravagance Andrew might indulge in' – a sharp rebuff which, it is claimed, induced Princess Beatrice, Queen Victoria's 67-year-old daughter and Prince Henry of Battenberg's widow, to make at least some temporary provision for the exiles. With neither his property, which seemed irretrievably confiscated, nor his army pay, Andrew possessed scant means. For the moment, he and his family received succour primarily from Princess Alice's relatives, an unenviable situation which the Prince was reluctant to accept. The more consistent of the benefactors would be the two Georges: Uncle George of Milford Haven and Andrew's brother, Prince George of Greece. But if Philip's cousin Alexandra is correct, George Milford Haven's contribution 'scarcely met the schooling expenses of the girls'. The second Marquess had inherited his father's title but no great wealth. Indeed, Prince Louis, retiring from the Royal Navy on a modest pension, had lived frugally compared with the standards of his social class. At one period his finances were so strained, it seems, that he and the Marchioness abandoned their home in the Isle of Wight, relying on the generosity of a former intimate, Miss Nora Kerr. The vicissitudes of life took their toll on Prince Louis in his later years and on one occasion, a contemporary, offering to give up his taxi to the Prince, received the reply: 'Oh, no, my dear fellow, I go on buses these days.'

Financial stringency, however, was not an anxiety of Prince George of Greece; he had married someone of immense affluence, Princess Marie Bonaparte – a great-granddaughter of Napoleon's brother Lucien. Paternal ancestry had endowed her with an eminent name, but it was from maternal ancestors that she inherited wealth; for the untitled Marie Blanc whom her father, Prince Roland Bonaparte, had married was the daughter of the founder of the Casino at Monte Carlo. It appears that, devoid of royal charisma, there had been a time when this Freudian advocate and enthusiast of psycho-analysis was a trifle embarrassing to the Glücksburgs. But circumstances can be realistic masters.

Prince Andrew had succeeded in some roundabout way in

getting money from an interest in farm property in Greece. This had been supplemented in January 1923 when his brother, King Constantine, died leaving Prince Andrew a small but now helpful bequest. Though accounts of straitened circumstances have perhaps been exaggerated, income – certainly by royal standards – does tend to have been of modest proportions. Thus to leave London for Paris and accept the generosity of the grand-daughter of François Blanc was a practical solution. In a sense the gold francs from the roulette tables indirectly aided Philip's family, especially in the early years of exile.

Philip's first home in France was a suite of rooms offered to Prince Andrew in a large mansion owned by Prince George and Princess Marie in the Rue Adolphe Ivan, close to the Bois de Boulogne. One version given for the family's eventual departure is that the quarters were much too cramped, but another implies that Prince Andrew could not afford the household needed. In any event, the family moved (and the premises have since been replaced by a modern apartment block). Uncle George and Aunt Marie lived in a house in the Rue du Mont Valérien, a substantial property at St Cloud, and in the grounds stood a lodge amid apple trees. This was to be the family's new address for some years, the one which Philip would always recall as home in early childhood. Discounting the faithful Roosie and a few retainers, this modest dwelling obviated the problem of keeping excessive staff which Prince Andrew could ill afford. He managed, however, to maintain a valet.

To imply that Philip was a sad, neglected child would be both false and absurd. He had the devotion of sisters years older than himself and the traits so marked today were apparently exhibited in childhood. He was a good-looking, ash-blond little extrovert who mixed with an air of assurance with all types of people. Throughout his life outdoor pursuits would appeal. This was apparent during visits – usually with Roosie and his sisters – to relatives in Germany. There were, for instance, the joyful hours with the Hesse family in Darmstadt, and the magic of their summer residence of Panka on the Baltic where he indulged his love of the sea.

Lingering in his mind long afterwards would be the memorable days with Aunt Sophie, ex-Queen of Greece, who had stayed one summer with her sister, the Landgravine of Hesse. There were trees to climb, the farm to explore and abundant opportunities for mischief. Panka was the rendezvous of uncles, aunts and cousins, and Philip's cousin Alexandra would write years later:

'One afternoon we had the entrancing idea of unbolting all the pig-stalls to see what would happen. To our disappointment everything went on just as before. The pigs went on grunting and browsing, paying no heed. It was almost as boring as if we were with the grown-ups on the lawn having tea ... To stir events up, Philip took a stick to the pigs – and then pandemonium broke loose with a fury of movement and sound. Squealing, screaming, freed from their sties, the pigs stampeded and scampered past the fodder barn towards the tea-lawn ... Between the elegant little chairs and tables the pigs rushed, upsetting trays and tea-things. I remember aunts and uncles screaming, shouting and running while dismayed servants rushed hither and thither, baffled by the swarming tide ... I remember shamelessly maintaining, in dire fear of punishment, that it was all Philip's idea and not mine. He saw to it, however, that I fully shared the blame.'

Perhaps the pig incident was an early illustration of his natural curiosity as to how things function. There were incidents, however, when his actions were nothing more than boyish exhibitionism and devilry. Philip was extremely fond of animals, especially a mongrel dog called 'Pompom'. This interest was extended to farm beasts, but in a different way. After quietly observing a farm worker, he once remarked: 'Perhaps the cow doesn't like to give milk, so it might be a good idea to take her mind off the milking. Why not feed her at the same time? She would be so happy eating she wouldn't worry about the milking, and she would then let you take as much as you like.'

Queen Marie was sometimes the host in Controcene near Bucharest. Philip's childhood recollections of Aunt Missy are of a radiant queen who, even when only the family were present for dinner, would don full evening dress and exquisite jewels, her hair agleam with a diamond tiara. Impressionable, too, was her story-telling to the children in her dressing-room before bedtime. In that childhood scene Philip's companion was his cousin Michael who, on the death of King Ferdinand of Rumania, had been proclaimed the sovereign under a regency. Sometimes during the intense summer heat the setting would change to the palace of Sinaia in the Transylvanian Alps, the home of Prince Andrew's niece, Queen Helen of Rumania.

When Philip was six years old he was admitted to the Mac-Jannet Country Day and Boarding School at St Cloud, a progressive kindergarten founded by a graduate of Tufts College, Massachusetts, for the children of rich Americans residing in France. To be taught in the MacJannet establishment was costly and in Philip's case the fees were defrayed by Philip's American aunt. The school was more widely known as The Elms because it existed in an old mansion of that name. Being close to the Rue du Mont Valérien, he was accompanied to school until he was old enough to cycle on a machine which he bought with pocket money. His uncle, the King of Sweden, sent him a pound as a present each Christmas, and this formed the basis of a fund to which others contributed. Though Philip was of royal status, he was among the poorer pupils at The Elms. Whether this was the outcome of necessity is not known, but both parents apparently emphasized the old-fashioned virtue of thrift; parental homilies advised him to save, advice which he accepted to the point at which others sometimes wrongly believed him to be mean.

Perhaps the most accurate insight into Prince Philip's character during boyhood is afforded by Mr Donald MacJannet himself. He described him as 'a rugged, boisterous boy, but always remarkably polite. He was full of energy and got along well with other children. He wanted to learn to do everything and asked at one time to be shown how to wait at table.' This assessment was confirmed by Miss Catherine Lewitsky, a junior teacher. On joining the school, she asked the boys in her class to introduce themselves. A flaxen-haired boy merely answered: 'Philip'. 'But Philip what?' asked Miss Lewitsky. 'Just Philip,' answered the boy, a trifle confused. 'But you must have another name,' insisted the teacher. 'Philip of Greece,' the boy blurted. Miss Lewitsky described him as being confident and authoritative.

Curiously, like his son Prince Charles a generation later, it was at his first school that he revealed his penchant for art. But it was mainly in sport in which he strove to distinguish himself. Even at that age he gave abundant evidence of his determination to achieve perfection. Whilst it was his mother who taught him the English language, he acquired from his father a reasonable knowledge of German, a language which he improved by associating with his German relatives. By residing in Paris, he spoke fluent French. It was also undoubtedly from Princess Alice that he gleaned most of the details of his ancestry – of the carefree, pre-war years at Darmstadt, the bitter-sweet life in Greece and the straitlaced Court of Queen Victoria. In later years, he would remark: 'If you want to know anything about the family, ask Mummy.'

A more detailed raconteur of Philip's maternal ancestry would be Uncle Dickie. In *The Mountbatten Lineage*, Lord Louis has not only explored the genealogical labyrinth with customary zest but applied his knowledge of naval signalling to explain complex cross-relationships.

Although he has never been stamped with the mystique of a British sovereign, Prince Philip at least has that indefinable aura which emanates from ancient lineage. The House of Hesse, of which the Battenbergs, or Mountbattens, are a ramification, can boast of an intriguing heritage meandering down to Charlemagne. To some extent the medieval chroniclers, portraying this historical figure, might almost be depicting Prince Philip in manhood: 'A typical German leader, over six feet in height, of superb athletic frame, great hunter and excellent swimmer; handsome with clear eyes, fair hair and a merry disposition.'

Archives in Darmstadt reveal that one Giselbert II, abducting the daughter of King Lothair of Lorraine, married her at Aquitaine. Since that marriage of Charlemagne's descendant the line has been fixed. Ancestral roots were planted in Louvain in Belgium and Nether-Lorraine, which was subsequently named Brabant. One cannot delve too deeply into Philip's family tree, but in these early centuries there was a marked leavening of kings: Otto the Great, Charles the Bald, Henry the Fowler and Hugh Capet of France. In this medieval tapestry one princess married Henry I of England and, on his death, William d'Aubigny, Earl of Arundel. Her brother Joceline took as wife the daughter of William de Percy, whose famous descendant Hotspur lives on in the words of Shakespeare. Richard Percy, their son, was among the twenty-five barons who ensured the fulfilment of England's greatest charter of liberties, Magna Carta.

War figures prominently in this massive cavalcade of Philip's forebears. For instance, Henry I of Brabant campaigned with Richard the Lionheart in the Third Crusade against Saladin, but his son Henry III the Magnanimous introduced a saint into the pedigree. He married twice, first to the granddaughter of the German Emperor Frederick Barbarossa, then to Sophie, daughter of Duke Louis IV of Thuringia and Elizabeth of Hungary – 'the mother of the poor'. Credited with the legendary miracle of turning bread into roses, she gave solace to lepers and kissed their sores. And when her brother-in-law drove her from Wartburg Castle on her husband's death, she entered a convent of the Franciscan Order but died when she was twenty-four. Sophie's canonization is remembered annually on a day in November when Catholics everywhere are exhorted 'to think little of worldly prosperity and to be ever gladdened by heavenly consolation'.

It was the sword, however, which enhanced the family's fortunes in the broad territories of Hesse. When only three, Elizabeth's grandson, King Henry the Child, inherited the lands of Thuringia and Hesse, enjoying for a while the vast ransom which his great-uncle, the German Emperor Henry Raspe, had exacted for liberating Richard, England's royal crusader. Eventually in the bloody struggles for the German imperial crown, Henry had to be satisfied with the title of Landgrave of Hesse. Yet even with this lesser dignity the family subscribed to Europe's history. In the Lutheran wars, Philip I joined others in leading the military forces of the Reformation. Imprisonment, however, followed his defiance of the Pope and the Emperor Charles V until his son-in-law, Prince Maurice of Saxony, released him with the aid of France. On his deathbed in 1567 Philip, the Protestant stalwart, shared his lands among his four sons. William, the eldest, received Hesse-Cassel; to Louis went Hesse-Marburg; Philip, the third son, was given Rhinefels; and Hesse-Darmstadt went to George, the youngest. When the Marburg and Rhinefels branches died out, their possessions were united with Hesse-Darmstadt, the line to which Prince Philip's mother belonged.

In time Protestantism would reap impressive rewards when, out of the intricacies of Prince Philip's family tree, emerged the original forebears of the House of Hanover. They would displace the last of the Catholic Stuarts on the British throne and Prince Philip himself would marry one of their descendants.

Over the years the Hesse family were as heterogeneous as any. Some were profligates, squandering the wealth they accumulated from outrageous taxes, but others were equally solicitous towards their people. Such were Louis the Peaceful and Hermann the Learned. Landgrave Louis V of Hesse-Darmstadt founded the University of Giessen and his son Frederick would be closely identified with British naval affairs. He commanded the galleys of the Knights of Malta against the Turks in 1640 and as captain-general of the island occupied the palace which in due course became Admiralty House. It is intriguing to realize that some three centuries later two Royal Naval descendants – Lord Mountbatten and Prince Philip – would serve in precisely the same quarters; indeed, it was from here that Lord Louis commanded the First Cruiser Squadron in the Mediterranean. A second prince, George, the younger son of the Landgrave Louis VI, commanded the Royal Marines at the capture of Gibraltar and was appointed its Governor in 1704.

One Landgrave, Louis IX, was undoubtedly eclipsed by his wife Caroline of the impecunious Court Zweibruecken. A person of high intellect, she applied her erudition towards creating Darmstadt into one of Germany's foremost intellectual centres

in the eighteenth century. To the 'Great Landgravine's' Court
travelled painters and sculptors, poets and philosophers. Present-
day descendants can be grateful; she restored and beautified
palaces which some of Prince Philip's relations now occupy.

The Hesse princes, however, no doubt in character with
their times, knew more about the science of war. In this princely
occupation they offered their services – particularly to Russia,
Austria and Prussia – as royal mercenaries. Competing with the
hired nationals of other countries, they displayed much skill in
selling their services for highly profitable return. In the eighteenth century the Grand Duke Charles of Hesse-Cassel, the
northern branch of the family line, actually introduced the practice of hiring out whole military formations. It was lucrative, for
Frederick II, his successor, supplied 22,000 Hessian troops –
many of them press-ganged into the army – to fight for Britain's
George III in the American War of Independence. On that
occasion the Hesse family fought on the losing side. But whatever the vicissitudes of life, on balance Hesse princes achieved
considerable self-aggrandisement. Such was the case of the
Hesse-Darmstadt line. During the Seven Years War, Landgrave Louis IX served in the Prussian army under Frederick
the Great but with the rise of Napoleon his son Louis X, allying
with the Rhine League, rallied to Bonaparte. Opportunism appears to have borne fruit, for 'the loyalties of the Hesse princes
during the Napoleonic wars veered like a windcock in a whirlwind'; the family profited by not being too rigid in its political
affiliations. Napoleon endowed Louis with estates confiscated
from the Church and a number of cities – among them Mainz
and Worms – which had previously been ruled by bishops.
Louis, with inflated pride, proclaimed himself Grand Duke,
expunging the lesser title of Landgrave. However, when Napoleon's fortunes began to wane he transferred his loyalties yet
again. At the Congress of Vienna, whereas most German
rulers who had allied with Bonaparte lost their thrones, Louis
adroitly placed himself among the victors. Ironically he was
rewarded with yet more land and the Powers confirmed his
title of Grand Duke Louis of Hesse and by Rhine.

It can be said in Louis's favour that he was a liberal ruler who gave Hesse a constitution and a parliamentary assembly and set the foundation for the German industrial revolution.

The second Grand Duke, Louis II, and his ailing wife Wilhelmina, daughter of Charles Louis, Margrave of Baden, were conspicuous more for their accumulation of dynastic power through marriages. But the clever scheming was really attributable to the ambitious Grand Duchess. Because her sisters had ascended the thrones of Russia, Sweden, Bavaria and Brunswick, she contrived grandiose marriage ties for her children. Unfortunately Wilhelmina was dying slowly of tuberculosis for which the Court physicians prescribed ice-cold baths 'to fight the fever and distemper'. Much blood letting enfeebled her further. It says much, therefore, for her tenacity that she endeavoured to secure ideal matches for her three sons and one daughter. Death had not overtaken her when her first-born, the later Grand Duke Louis III, married Princess Mathilde, daughter of King Louis of Bavaria and sister of that ill-fated Otto, the future King of Greece.

Wilhelmina knew that a marriage had been arranged between Charles, her second son, and the granddaughter of King Frederick William II of Prussia. Five years after Wilhelmina's death, her daughter Marie, then sixteen, married the Tsarevitch of Russia, the future Tsar Alexander II. Her brother Alexander, who was one year older, would elope with a young ward of the Russian Empress. He would be cashiered and, as described later, from this romance the Battenberg, or Mountbatten, line would originate.

Set against this grandiose lineage, Prince Philip's childhood in France looks a trifle out of character. Money was by no means lavished upon him. Indeed, on the authority of his cousin Alexander, who was conversant with Philip's activities in those days – 'Neither Aunt Alice nor Uncle Andrew believed in making everything easy.' Pocket money had to spent wisely, especially if one accepts the raincoat incident. Due to a heavy downpour, he was detained at school one afternoon because he had no raincoat. Philip brightly explained that he was saving his money to buy one. Perhaps, he is alleged to have told his teacher, he would have the means to buy one the following week.

To what extent Philip was left 'to his own devices' in child hood, it is hard to say. Maybe it was no more than that of most children. True, much of Princess Alice's time was concentrated on 'Hellas', a little boutique. The story that Philip's mother ran an antique shop in a struggle with poverty is entirely false. Her modest enterprise, in which she sold Greek embroideries, tapestries and other articles, was essentially a charitable organization to help Greek expatriates. It drew wealthy patrons, including visiting Americans, some of whom were sent by her sister-in-law, Princess Christopher in New York. Now and then Prince Nicholas – who with Princess Helen and their family had joined the community of exiles in Paris – would present one of his paintings. While in exile in Switzerland with Philip's parents, he had rented a small room for a studio and hired an art teacher for six hours daily. These art lessons were to prove a valuable investment. In Paris Prince Andrew's brother had resorted to art as a means of livelihood and pictures signed by *Nicholas le Prince* created their own market.

Like her sister-in-law Princess Alice, Princess Helen organized a charity – in this case a children's home for orphaned Russians. Princess Helen had been appalled and heartbroken at the plight of Russian refugees in Paris. Some were so destitute that they scoured the dustbins, and lacking food some perished during the severe winters, leaving unwanted children to roam the streets. In their humanity Philip's uncle and aunt opened a children's home in a country house at St Germain-en-Laye, they themselves living in a small flat in the old Trocadero. Marina, their youngest daughter, sometimes visited St Cloud to the delight of her cousin Philip. Her arrival might signify trips to Paris to see marionettes, Punch and Judy shows and other exciting amusements. Being some years his senior, Philip regarded Marina more as an aunt, and from that time until her death, a close friendship persisted.

It is not unlikely that at this period Philip was experiencing the uneasiness of insecurity. The minds of three of his four sisters were beginning to dwell on husbands, and the domestic happiness that prevailed in the Trocadero flat was somewhat absent from the house in St Cloud. Between Prince Andrew and Princess Alice there had grown a tension which was apparent to any intelligent child. Perhaps it is an accurate assessment that the parents had never been wholly compatible, but the strain of the events in Greece had worsened this domestic flaw. The mortifying ordeal of the Athens trial had scarred Prince Andrew's mind, leaving an intense feeling of bitterness. It is on record that he 'was intractable, his equanimity in tatters'. Writing of Prince Andrew, Air Vice-Marshal Arthur S. Gould Lee, who had the co-operation of members of the Greek Royal Family, revealed that Prince Andrew was 'unable to forgive the way in which, after long years of honest military service, he had been subjected to public insult and indignity for the sins of others'. It is probable too that Princess Alice, now in the grip of religious self-expression and contemplation, bewildered and perhaps even angered him. Tolerance and sympathy were proably absent. The parents certainly contrasted in character. Prince Andrew is generally described as having been gay and highly intelligent with a bias, if anything, towards controversy whereas Princess Alice was of an ingenuous, uncomplicated disposition, and all the time there were the unshakable demands of her religion.

The upshot was a gradual drifting apart of the parents. There was no official announcement, merely the tacit decision to go their separate ways. That Prince Philip maintained his own equanimity and emerged as a brilliant, outstanding man of his times can only suggest that it was due to inherent qualities and subsequent potent yet benevolent influences. On one point both parents were in total agreement: Prince Philip must never be exposed to the sort of outrage which Prince Andrew had experienced; he must therefore be trained for a completely different life. Alice's widowed mother and brothers, George and Louis, were conscious of the strained environment at St Cloud, and the members of Prince Andrew's own family – as well as mutual friends – were alive to the pending breach and its probable impact on Prince Philip. One of Princess Alice's friends Madame Foufounis, a Greek exile, sympathetically gave him hours of happiness. Philip first enjoyed her hospitality while she was residing at her lovely country house, the Villa Georges, with its own farm, just outside Marseilles. There he enjoyed the companionship of her children – Ria, Hélène (today Madame Hélène Cordet) and their brother Ianni – and when they were taken for periods to Borck Plage near Le Touquet, Philip, Roosie and his sisters would sometimes accompany them, too.

Recalling those vignettes of childhood, Madame Cordet has revealed that, although she liked Philip, she was worried by the fuss her mother, by then a widow, made of him. To Philip's amusement, in these moments of jealousy she exposed her feelings. But 'we had a wonderful time playing soldiers, growing vegetables and fruit on our little plot of land (given to us so that we would keep out of mischief), and feeding the animals on the farm. Philip's great distraction was cleaning the pigsties'.

When she was seven years old, Ria was enclosed in plaster due to a hip complaint; she would remain lying that way for the next five years. After the initial bitterness Ria accepted her illness philosophically. One day while at Berck, a friend brought toys for all except the unfortunate Ria. 'I didn't get you anything because you can't play like the others,' he explained rather insensitively. Philip looked at Ria who was endeavouring to suppress her tears, then hurried to his room. Minutes later he returned, his arms clutching his own toys as well as the new one. 'All this is yours!' he said, placing them on Ria's bed. He was four years old at the time.

In Berck, Philip would often sit beside Ria's bed chatting with her. No amount of luring, Madame Cordet has explained, would make him budge. He sat there quietly, but at other times the noise in the house was devastating. There was the regular spanking. Once Philip and Ianni broke an enormous vase. While Ianni was getting his beating from Miss Macdonald, a formidable Scottish governess, called 'Aunty', Philip disappeared. Suddenly his frightened blue eyes were seen behind french windows and in a panic he cried: 'Nanny, let's clear.' Aunty promptly descended on Philip. He straightened himself, looked her squarely in the eye, and said: 'I'll get my spanking from Roosie, thank you.'

There was resourcefulness, too, in those tender years. After lunch during the hot summer Ianni would go into the reception room, pick up some of the Persian rugs, then he and Philip would take their siesta on them in the garden. One afternoon the boys vanished, and so did the rugs. For an hour the house and farm were in a turmoil, but the boys could not be found. Suddenly someone rang the bell at one of the garden gates. A woman explained that the boys were going from door to door, with the carpets on their shoulders, trying to sell them.

Childhood also had its painful moments. Pretending that they were keeping a dental appointment, Ianni and Philip went off to see a circus instead. The young Hélène, mad with fury at being deceived, turned on them both, her eyes blazing. Ianni ran quickly out of reach but Philip merely stood as if fascinated by her anger. She grabbed him by his very blond hair, not letting go until finally she was left with tufts in each hand. (Prince Philip has since left a record of those nostalgic times. Many of the Foufounis's snapshots are in safe keeping in the Royal Archives at Windsor.)

Philip's future was determined largely by his parents, his maternal grandmother, two uncles and a sister. Not only would they direct his upbringing but, wittingly or not, help to pattern his destiny. Certainly one member of this group, Uncle Dickie, would to some degree stamp his influence on his nephew in the malleable years. Moreover, it would be in the invigorating, progressive environment of Lord Mountbatten's household that his nephew would burgeon in a modern world.

Experience had taught that Britain was the securest haven for royalty. It was agreed, therefore, that Philip should live with his grandmother in England, and that Uncle George should serve as guardian. But her apartments at Kensington Palace were too restricting for a boisterous boy. He bought a toy saxophone from a store in Kensington High Street but was discouraged from using it; the noise might disturb the peace of his great-aunt Princess Beatrice, their neighbour. The two extremes of age did not blend. Thus Philip, who came to London at the age of eight, was subsequently installed at Lynden Manor, the home of Uncle George. Philip was already familiar with this

Thames-side home near Maidenhead and more appropriately
he had the companionship of his cousin David, his senior by
two years. Here was greater freedom. The boys could satisfy
their exuberance in the grounds, especially in a garden barn
used primarily as a badminton court.

With Prince Andrew's consent, it was agreed to send Philip
to Cheam School. Already there was a firm association between
this exclusive establishment and the Mountbatten family. It
had originated in 1914 when Prince Louis of Battenberg, then
the First Sea Lord, had been agreeably surprised by the aplomb
of two midshipmen. Learning that they were ex-pupils of Cheam,
he decided that it should be the preparatory school for his son
George. The oldest preparatory school in England, with a
foundation dating to the reign of Charles I, its boys were matri-
culating at Oxford and Cambridge even during the Civil War.
In 1665, when Charles II had been restored to the throne, the
Rev George Aldritch, who maintained a little school in London
for aristocratic sons, fled from the Great Plague and with his
noble scholars found sanctuary in the Surrey market town of
Cheam. Sharing a house called Whitehall in the High Street,
Cheam School's reputation grew and many of the affluent regis-
tered the names of their sons at birth. By 1719 it occupied new
premises in Cheam, among elm trees and thirteen acres of
land. The railway station and encroaching urbanization caused
the school to uproot itself yet again – in 1931, this time to
Headley on the Berkshire Downs, but retaining the name of
Cheam.

This ancient school has had a chequered history. When William Gilpin purchased it in 1752, he brought reform. To the
eighteenth-century mind the technique was to beat learning into
boys. Gilpin, however, was loath to flog, deciding instead on a
specific punishment for a particular offence. Fines or detention
in varying degrees, and physical exercise, were the fundamentals
of his code. Only in the extremest of cases was the birch wielded,
and then rarely. Gilpin, who may have been the model for
Smollett's schoolmaster in *Peregrine Pickle*, was otherwise
known as 'Dr Syntax'.

Sometimes it is known as the Tabor School – a name derived

from its mid-nineteenth-century headmaster. Tabor was highly sensitive to rank. A peer was addressed as 'my darling child', he referred to the son of a peer as 'my dear child' and a commoner was a mere 'my child'. It is interesting to speculate how he would have addressed Prince Philip.

Not unexpectedly, distinguished names are inscribed in Cheam's register. That of Thomas Pepys, cousin of the industrious Samuel, the diarist, is there. So too is that of Lord Randolph Churchill who, according to Sir Winston, his even more illustrious son, was 'most kindly treated and quite content'. One can visualize Lord Randolph, accompanied by the future Lords Donoughmore and Aberdeen bowling along at Cheam in a four-in-hand. The school's ex-pupils also included two former viceroys of India, Lord Willingdon and Lord Hardinge of Penshurst, as well as two Speakers of the House of Commons: Henry Addington (later Viscount Sidmouth), who by means of the Treaty of Amiens ended the war with France in 1802; and Colonel Clifton-Brown (subsequently Viscount Ruffside). Lord Dunsany, the Irish writer, and Sir Ian Hamilton, military commander-in-chief at the disastrous Gallipoli landing, were also at Cheam. Prince Philip and his cousin David Milford Haven were among the last of the scholars before the migration from Surrey.

When Prince Philip was an inmate of Cheam the staff did not believe in pampering their pupils. Clothes were kept in wicker baskets called 'Dog baskets'. In the dormitories the centuries-old beds were hard, the wooden floor uncarpeted. And no one was foolishly squeamish over corporal punishment. At the tercentenary celebrations in 1947 Prince Philip introduced Princess Elizabeth, his future wife, to a former headmaster, the Rev Harold Taylor, remarking: 'This is my late headmaster, who used to cane me.' Philip, like the other boys, made his bed and was inspected each morning for tidiness. Discipline was the hall-mark of the Cheam curriculum, and the value he attached to Cheam is reflected in the fact that he chose it for his son, Prince Charles.

In his three years at Cheam the high-spirited Philip distinguished himself in athletics by becoming the school's diving

champion, tying for first place in the high jump and impressing
on the soccer field. Athletics meant much to him, but in the
academic sphere at this stage he was mediocre. In all his
studies, Philip was most competent at history. He won a prize
for French yet the achievement was scarcely meritorious considering that he had lived in France; the other boys were de-
cidedly at a disadvantage.

Holidays were invariably spent at Lynden Manor where he
was accepted like a son. It is sometimes suggested that Lord
Louis Mountbatten exercised the most pronounced influence
on Prince Philip during this period. In later years this was
true but there was no substance for this claim in boyhood. At
this stage George, the second Marquess of Milford Haven, was
the mentor who wisely counselled his nephew. Somewhat eclipsed by his forceful younger brother, it is not generally appreciated that, although he left little imprint on his times, he was a
naval officer of remarkable abilities who was generally accepted
as the inheritor of his father's brilliance. To his nimble mind
everything appears to have been absorbed with astonishing
ease; for instance, 'tactical orders, dashed off without pause or
after-thought, were considered a model for naval procedure'.
The influence of George Milford Haven had a vital effect in
shaping Prince Philip's character. Uncle George possessed in
full measure the Mountbatten charm and, in his particular case,
an endearing amiability. It was mental balm for the boy more
accustomed to the tensions at St Cloud. It is highly likely that
the Marquess's own love for the Navy must have imbued his
nephew likewise, but although it has been asserted that he
'nurtured the boy's inclinations towards a career in the Royal
Navy', Philip has since minimized this. Correcting a miniature
biography which was issued officially, he wrote: 'In choosing
a career in one of the services he was following the traditions
of both sides of his family. Both his grandfathers served at sea.
His father was a career officer in the Greek Army, and both his
father's and his mother's brothers served in the Navy.'

And yet in those impressionable years, during what were
akin to paternal talks, he heard much about naval life, including a vivid account of the action at Jutland. Uncle George had

served on that dramatic day in *New Zealand*, commanding the two forward 12-inch guns which became over-heated through intense firing. (Lord Louis Mountbatten has claimed that the turret commanded by George Milford Haven 'fired more heavy shells at the enemy than any turret of any other ship on either side in World War One or World War Two'.) George, a gifted technician, was in his natural environment on the deck of a ship, but the limited inheritance and naval pay were inadequate to maintain Lynden and his wife Nada with her Russian grand ducal tastes. Philip was still at Cheam when, in 1932, having attained the rank of captain, his uncle resigned to seek richer prizes in commerce – first on the New York Stock Exchange and then representing in Britain the Sperry Gyroscope Company of America. There was a sprinkling of directorships, too.

Meanwhile at St Cloud, Philip's family had broken up; his four sisters had married, reviving the close intertwining of German princely families and the British Royal Family in Victoria's time. To their dismay, within a decade war would place Prince Philip and his sisters on conflicting sides. Sophie, the youngest, then only sixteen, and known in the family as 'Tiny', was the first to leave France, marrying the tall, 30-year-old Prince Christopher of Hesse. Her marriage recalled memories of the First World War, for Christopher was the youngest brother of Prince Maximilian of Hesse who, as a nineteen-year-old lieutenant in the Prussian Death's Head Hussars, had been fatally wounded in Flanders by British cavalry. At a British hospital at Bailleul, this great-grandson of Queen Victoria had requested a doctor to send a locket to his mother in Germany, but fate had intervened. Three days after Prince Maximilian's death, the doctor himself was killed; the hospital was blasted by a German shell. Fortunately the doctor had written a note, and the locket, despatched to his widow in England, was duly received by Queen Mary. In time Philip's aunt, Princess Louise of Battenberg, sent the locket to Maximilian's mother, Princess Margaret of Hesse.

To the embarrassment of Prince Philip and the Mountbattens in Britain, three years after his marriage Prince Christopher –

known in the family as 'Cri' – came under Hitler's spell; he accepted Naziism in its entirety, joining Himmler's staff in Berlin. Some German aristocrats were enmeshed by Hitlerism through circumstance, but it is not difficult to detect where Prince Christopher's sympathies lay. Volunteering for flying duties in Göring's Luftwaffe, the pilot-prince dropped his bombs during raids on London. But death also claimed him in Italy in a similar sortie. Sophie was a widow at twenty-nine with four young children and a fifth born after her husband's death in 1944. Eventually she married Prince George of Hanover augmenting her family with three more children. Her husband, the Duke of Brunswick, was also the Duke of Cumberland until an Act of Parliament deprived him of the title in 1917. Prince George was therefore in direct descent of the Hanoverian kings of England. Another illustration of the entanglements of war occurred in 1961 when his brother, Prince Ernest August, claimed rights as a British national. He succeeded, but the Master of the Rolls observed: '... it seems an extraordinary thing that a man who fought against this country could come along and say that he was a British subject; if he is right he would appear to have committed high treason during the war.'

All Prince Philip's sisters married within a year – in 1930-1. Sophie's wedding was followed by that of Cecile to her first cousin once removed, the Grand Duke George Donatus of Hesse. Margarita, the eldest, married Prince Gottfried von Hohenlohe-Langenburg, a grandson of Prince Alfred of Edinburgh (and thus the great-grandson of Queen Victoria), and Theodora became the wife of Berthold, Margrave of Baden, a union that would rebound on Prince Philip himself. Theodora's father-in-law, Prince Max of Baden, had been the last Chancellor of Imperial Germany. As such the Kaiser, desperately anxious to save his throne, had prevailed upon him to seek from Lloyd George, President Wilson and Clemenceau an 'armistice of honour'. But Prince Max, a humanitarian of liberal outlook, starkly conscious that only the Kaiser's withdrawal and the destruction of his Prussian military clique could win peace and true democracy for Germany, proclaimed the Kaiser's abdication before the German monarch had been warned. Prince Max – ranted against by immoderate German nationalists as 'the Red Prince' – made way for the Socialist Ebert and after proclaiming the republic surrendered to the Allies.

Retiring to Schloss Salem, his estate on the forested shores of Lake Constance, Prince Max founded a revolutionary type of school in a wing of his gargantuan castle. His objective was to create a new élite – a new German intelligentsia from the wreckage of war cleansed of Junker militarism. Incorporating ideas from the British public schools system – the secret, he believed, of the success of British imperialist power – he combined them with the thoroughness of German teaching.

As time would confirm, the person he chose to supervise this democratic nursery – an astute professor named Dr Kurt Hahn – would become a dominant figure in Prince Philip's life. His political adviser during Prince Max's Chancellorship, Hahn had later joined the German delegation at Versailles and collaborated in drafting the new constitution of the Weimar Republic. A Rhodes Scholar at Christ Church, Oxford, before the First World War and steeped in progressive ideas, Hahn originally strove for an 'élite of enlightened leaders'. The school began in 1920 with four pupils, including Theodora's future husband, but by the early 'thirties it ranked high among the foremost educational establishments in Europe. There was a preponderance of boys from aristocratic and wealthy families until Hahn introduced a leavening of the middle class, charging fees according to parental means. One essential was to cleanse the sons of any idea of the privilege of high birth and to concentrate on self-reliance and self-expression. Hahn, who described Salem as a school where 'the sons of the powerful' could be 'emancipated from the prison of privilege', was also impressed by the stamina bred in British public schools. Endorsing the principles of Dr Thomas Arnold of Rugby, above all, he emphasized the twin developments of physique and the intellect. Pupils were taught to accept life philosophically and, to stress its virtues with almost monastic discipline, Hahn even ordered regular periods of silence and self-contemplation. Against this he demanded and stimulated strenuous physical training, often in the spirit of adventure. Sports were catered for but never practised in the manner of their British counterparts. 'We dethrone sport,' remarked Hahn, believing that if games were not looked upon as paramount they were played more keenly. The end products were intended to be the enlightened leaders in politics and diplomacy, industry and commerce to foster Germany's much needed revival.

Theodora enthused over her father-in-law's venture, dissipating any family doubts that Salem would be ideal for Philip on leaving Cheam. Philip himself never accepted the decision with zest, disliking his removal from a pleasant existence in England. He was twelve years old, tousle-haired and rather unkempt when he arrived at Salem, a disarming grin exposing a broken tooth sustained when he collided while playing hockey on roller skates with his cousin David. Prince Philip would need good humour to maintain his buoyancy in the next twelve months. Salem did not cater for the personal comfort of the four hundred scholars in the old, four-storey monastic buildings that ranged round three great quadrangles. The corridors were echoing and chilly but Hahn's aim was 'not to turn out tame deer but to give the boys opportunities for self-discovery and make them meet with triumph and defeat'.

Prince Philip's reaction during three terms at Salem is greatly reflected in personal achievement. He fared rather badly both in studies and the sports to which he was normally addicted. He lacked the characteristic effort to excel and seemed quite content to tackle the daily routine with the minimum amount of effort. Not that Salem allowed anyone to escape exercise. As Kurt Hahn recorded, before breakfast 'all the boys ran slowly for 400 yards, preferably on their toes. All boys skipped in the morning and did physical drill at night. Many climbed a rope each day. Four times a week, all the year round, academic studies in the morning had a 45-minute break for the practice of running, jumping and javelin throwing.' That was only one facet of the Spartan life; Hahn's curriculum did not allow for physical weaklings, and all the boys underwent hard labour, engaging in such tasks as heavy building and agriculture.

It is interesting to speculate on what course Prince Philip's career would have taken had he continued to live in the country of his Battenberg ancestors. It is doubtful if he would have been the First Gentleman of the Realm in Britain. In any event, certain events – much to his relief – forced him back to England. Philip had joined Salem for the winter term of 1932–3 and by now Nazi jackboots were strutting more arrogantly in the streets. Hitler had come to power as the German Chancellor, making his spurious promises, deceiving both the gullible and those anxious to appease. Heinrich Himmler had embarked on his sadistic baiting of the Jews, many of whom had fled. An ominous note rang throughout the Fatherland, but for none more threateningly than men like Hahn. Defined as 'a decadent Jewish corrupter of German youth', Hahn was arrested and jailed on a trumped-up charge of being a Communist. Had the incident occurred a few years later, when Hitler seized total power, nothing could have saved Hahn from a dreadful fate. But speedy intervention by Prince Berthold – now serving as headmaster in Hahn's absence – backed by vehement protests from scholars throughout Europe, as well as a direct appeal by Ramsay MacDonald, Britain's Prime Minister, finally induced President Hindenburg to release him. Escaping from the Nazis, Hahn quit Salem for the safety of Britain.

For a while Salem was allowed to function under Prince Berthold, but the precepts of the system were now threatened by Nazi ideology. At one point, so it is said, the Nazis conceived the idea of adapting Salem into an academy for the Hitler youth. But the staff – defiantly adhering to Hahn's principles – opposed Nazi control until the school was finally closed. Prince Philip had already left Germany before that day. Utterly contemptuous of the Nazi doctrine (an attitude which he made no effort to conceal) he scoffed at Nazi posturing – the heel-clicking and the outstretched salute. To him it was ludicrous – the butt of amusement. Hence the day a hostile SS officer furiously demanded that Prince Berthold should summarily punish a fair-haired pupil. And when Storm Troopers gave the Hitler salute in the market square of nearby Uberlingen and Philip roared with laughter, asking if the men with upraised arms were seeking 'to be excused', his stay in Germany was considered to be rather precarious. Casting caution aside, he mocked the Brown-shirts' goose-step and ridiculed the Nazi salute. Theodora and Berthold realized that Philip's detestation of Naziism might endanger him as well as themselves. After a family discussion, it seemed safer for all concerned that Philip should return to the care of his elder uncle in England.

Out of the ruins of the Salem experiment would emerge Gordonstoun. When Dr Hahn fled from persecution, men of influence rallied to his aid, among them Mr Claude Elliott (then headmaster of Eton), Lord Tweedsmuir (the author John Buchan and, subsequently Governor-General of Canada), Professor G. M. Trevelyan (the historian), Lord Allen of Hurtwood, Dr William Temple (Archbishop of Canterbury) and Admiral Sir Herbert Richmond. Dr Hahn had been fascinated by the rugged grandeur of Morayshire on walks during vacations from Oxford. It was there that he now leased turreted Gordonstoun and three hundred heather-clad acres overlooking the Moray Firth. Not far from Elgin, the estate had been the property of the Gordon-Cummings family, whose ancestor, Sir William, the fourteenth baronet, had been involved in the baccarat scandal in 1890. The Prince of Wales (the future Edward VII) had dealt the cards at Sir William's Tranby Croft estate and in the legal action that ensued Gordon-Cummings had been accused of cheating. That was not the whole of the notorious past of the Gordonstoun owners. On one side of the attractive mansion, with its pepper-pot turrets and balustraded roof, stands the Round Square, a circular lawn hemmed in by the stable quarter. Here, many years ago the laird of the day was said to be in communion with the devil. Near by is one of the four pigeon-cotes that the same laird constructed, labouring under the misguided belief that to keep pigeons would guarantee the death of a wife.

In the summer of 1934 Dr Hahn resurrected his school amid the pines and Sitka spruce of Scotland. With him was a nucleus of pupils – one of whom was Prince Philip – and a few masters, including Mr Robert Chew, a Cambridge graduate, who had taught mathematics for four years at Salem. Then the deputy headmaster, he now supervised mountain climbing and became

Philip's housemaster, the 'house' being a group of huts christened Windmill Lodge. (Here Prince Charles would come a generation later.)

While in Germany Hahn had been accused of trying to anglicize German education. This was not true. His desire to foster physique and the intellect, applying both in the service of society, was derived from the ancient Greeks. Hahn drew considerably from Plato's *Republic*. In Sparta the nobility had arranged for their sons to live and study together in groups from the age of seven, each group being supervised by a master with a prefect as leader (similarly at Gordonstoun a master, assisted by a head boy – Prince Philip fulfilled these duties at Windmill Lodge – would be in charge of each house). In these select communities training was rigorous and even harsh, but it yielded amazing standards of endurance. Spartanism as encouraged by Dr Hahn, however, was less demanding, his aim being to stimulate in his pupils powers of self-discipline, pitting their skill against the elements both on land and sea.

It is somewhat singular that a Prince of Greece should be taught in a Scottish public school where the inspiration was ancient Greece. Philip had disliked Salem intensely. It was not the exacting duties that had depressed him, but the overtones of Naziism and the humourless militant youth. But the physical tasks at Gordonstoun were more palatable, and more in keeping with one of the original precepts at Salem. Centuries ago the Cistercians had thrived at Salem, administering to the needs of the neighbourhood. This altruism was rekindled by Kurt Hahn and his pupils. Hahn dovetailed school activities with those of the local people. Philip and his fellows offered their services in the small boatyards on the Moray coast and assisted in the nearby smithy and Coastguards.

Mixing with humble Scottish folk, Prince Philip 'overcame the disadvantages of his royal birth'. It was beneficial for the future, too. No British prince – certainly not in this century – had ever integrated himself so closely in his youth with ordinary people. At school he worked and played with boys from contrasting social backgrounds, and some of his friends were fishermen and their families in the nearby village of Hopeman.

Such experience would be helpful when mixing with all shades of society as the consort of a queen.

For the endurance tests, which were intended to promote initiative and keep the body fit and strong, Dr Hahn had the natural assets of mountains and sea. Philip preferred the latter; he disliked walking, and mountains smacked too much of the wearisome treks experienced at Salem. Helping to make and repair boats – and, better still, learning to sail them in Hopeman harbour – stirred the brine in the blood of a youth with Viking ancestry. Gordonstoun possessed a number of boats – and finally a schooner – and to train his charges in sailing, Hahn engaged Commander Lewty, a retired Royal Naval officer, as instructor.

From sailing in the rough waters of the Moray Firth, Philip graduated to voyages to the Shetlands and the Outer Hebrides and even Norway. Unaffected by sea-sickness himself, on the latter enterprise Prince Philip had also to grapple with boisterous seas as cook; his squeamish shipmates could not tolerate the smells of the tiny galley. 'He is a cheerful shipmate,' reported Commander Lewty, 'very conscientious in carrying out both major and minor duties, thoroughly trustworthy and unafraid of dirty and arduous work.'

Prince Philip was a pioneer pupil at Gordonstoun in every sense, actually helping to convert old stable quarters into dormitories and classrooms. There was also a pig-sty to build. But no matter how laborious or irksome the daily tasks, Philip, like the other pupils, had to complete his 'confessionals' each night. These were the daily admissions, if necessary, of any infringement of school rules. Had he eaten sweets between meals? Did he walk when he was supposed to run? And so on. No master ever examined these charts. The pupil was placed on trust to honour his commitments and if he was evasive or lied, then the punishment was expected to be a nagging conscience. This may appear to be fatuous when set against the permissive and jejune attitudes of modern times, but in realistic terms it bred honesty and trained the individual to discipline and supervise himself. No human community, however, is wholly devoid of sporadic misbehaviour and 'Punishments One to Six' were sometimes enforced commensurate to the gravity of the offence. Numbers one to five were restricted to strenuous walks; number six inevitably decreed a visit to the headmaster. As punishment, ostensibly the walks seem to be rather ridiculous, yet the reverse was the case. The length of the walk varied according to the degree of misconduct, but it was imperative to complete it before the compulsory daily run of a mile at 7 a.m. Thus a boy rose at six (or earlier), made his bed and arranged his locker and, after the regulation cold shower, set off (sometimes in snow or driving rain) to atone. Should the length be four miles or more, the culprit made expiation for his misdemeanour at the fatiguing rate of a mile in less than fifteen minutes. Having made reparations almost to the point of collapse, there was still the customary mile to complete.

To Prince Philip the Hahn system was stimulating and challenging. His pliant character responded. Hahn himself would write:

'When Philip came to Gordonstoun his most marked trait was his undefeatable spirit. He felt the emotions of both joy and sadness deeply, and the way he looked and the way he moved indicated what he felt. That even applied to the minor disappointments inevitable in a schoolboy's life. His laughter was heard everywhere. He had inherited from his Danish family the capacity to derive great fun from small incidents. In his school work he showed a lively intelligence. In community life, once he had made a task his own, he showed meticulous attention to detail and pride of workmanship which was never content with mediocre results.'

As a perfectionist, Prince Philip has always been scornful of the facile and the second best, yet at school he himself was not a paragon of all the virtues. Hahn judged him to be 'often naughty, never nasty', and he also noted at times Prince Philip's impatience and intolerance towards others. Apparently he was compelled to learn horsemanship – a punishment from which he subsequently reaped pleasure on the polo field – because he waspishly belittled others who favoured a pastime which then had no appeal for him.

But Prince Philip would never claim to aspire to saintly virtues. His over-riding quality – almost to the point of obsession – is to do everything he attempts superbly well. Impatience with others less fastidious has been known to flare, but the anger is just as swiftly quelled. At school half-measures were anathema to him once his enthusiasm had been stimulated by some practical objective. Yet Dr Hahn once detected passive resistance when a Coastguard project was first mooted. Whether or not Prince Philip considered the scheme as something nebulous, or whether he suspected it to be an act of purification, has never been disclosed. But on being assured that the Coastguard service would include it in its network, even paying for the cost of a telephone, Philip went ahead with vigour. Organizing a working party, the post was built, despite the vagaries of autumn gales, in readiness for winter. Since then the station, commanding a long stretch of wild Morayshire coast, has been manned by Gordonstoun boys at the announcement of gale warnings.

During vacations there was no parental home to which Prince Philip could return, a domestic loss which one cannot minimize. It is hard to accept that the absence of a family welcome did not make him ponder at that time. To what, if any, extent it created an unhappy influence only he can say. Against this, there could be few boys who had access to such a variety of social contacts. During the years of schooling, Lynden Manor was about the nearest approach to a genuine home. It had the added attraction that during holidays there was a companion for Prince Philip – Uncle George's son, David Milford Haven. Both were temperamentally in tune, enjoying the same pleasures and adventures. Typical was the secret nocturnal boat journey down the Thames to climb to a roof skylight and watch the dance sessions at an hotel. In childhood Philip had long shown a tendency to climb. There was, for instance, the incident at Kensington Palace when, defying the strictures of a police officer, he refused to come down from the roof. Philip, however, was swiftly subdued by the stern reproaches of his maternal grandmother.

For vacations there was also the sumptuous Park Lane

home of Uncle Dickie and Aunt Edwina. Initially it was Brook House, the mansion which Sir Ernest Cassel, the international financier and Edwina's grandfather, had purchased from Lord Tweedmouth. Vast sums had been lavished on its renovations and decorations, but Sir Ernest's taste, it seems, was not in keeping with his wealth; it acquired the description of 'a vulgar palace'. About eight hundred tons of Tuscany marble came from Michelangelo's quarries at Sarravezza to line the main hall and staircase, and even the kitchens. Rare Canadian marble and lapis lazuli subscribed to the magnificence. The library was furnished entirely in cherrywood, adorned with oval cameos of black Wedgwood. Turkish baths added to the Eastern splendour. The dining-room, enhanced by an arched ceiling and panelled in oak, was lit by Roman lamps of antique bronze. One of Prince Philip's earliest glimpses – and perhaps the first – of Brook House was at the age of four when, hiding beneath one of the enormous beds, he was pulled out despite lusty protests. But the Mountbatten residence with which he was more familiar was Uncle Dickie's next London home. Brook House, costing £17,000 a year for its upkeep, was reduced to rubble, and in May 1933 the site was sold to Messrs Coutts and Co., the royal bankers. Gone was the mansion where Sir Ernest Cassel had entertained King Edward VII. In its place rose a block of flats crowned by Britain's first penthouse. Described at that time as London's most spectacular home, this two-storey apartment afforded a striking contrast to the hard beds and bare wooden floors with which Prince Philip was familiar at Gordonstoun. If necessary, the five reception rooms (equipped with soundproof partitions that could be concealed in the walls) were quickly adapted into a ballroom or cinema. The upper floor comprised two major suites with guest rooms and bathrooms. The lower floor embraced the nursery wing (with its own kitchen), the long gallery and reception rooms, and the servants' quarters. Most probably Prince Philip was more impressed by Uncle Dickie's personal rooms which, in their comparative austerity, bore the atmosphere of a naval ship. Here Lord Mountbatten had given generous play to his inventive mind, for here and there were examples of his own particular gadgetry. Prince Philip has always been fascinated by mechanics and an automatic lift at a private entrance in Upper Brook Street never failed to intrigue. He enthused over the lift's incredible speed and the secret floor switch which, operated by the butler's weight, allowed the doors to open.

During the Gordonstoun phase, Philip also made visits to his sisters in Germany. Happily, quite often it would be the occasion for a reunion between father and son. Prince Andrew had continued to live in Paris, and for news of Philip he relied on a constant flow of photographs and letters. What impressed Prince Philip's sisters was the amazing resemblance between their father and brother. Though living far apart and seeing each other only rarely, their mannerisms and mode of walking were identical, as well as strong physical resemblances. Each had an irresistible desire to play pranks, and a spontaneous wit. (Though physically unalike, today some of those traits are again reproduced in Prince Philip's son, Prince Charles.)

There would be a further reunion – this time with an element of the macabre – in November 1936. A plebiscite had restored the monarchy in Greece. During the republican era Philip's uncle and aunt, King Constantine and Queen Sophie, and grandmother, Queen Olga, had died in exile and it was now agreed to take them from a crypt in Florence and bury them in the royal burial ground at Tatoi. Before that they were to lie in state for six days in Athens Cathedral.

The solemnity of the occasion did not destroy the joy of a family reunion. The persons concerned had been dead long enough to permit some festive spirit. Aunts, uncles and cousins drove through the streets – now decked with flags which would soon yield to drapes of mourning – to the cheers of the people. Prince Philip's relatives arrived in such numbers that they occupied completely the city's foremost hotel, the Grand Bretagne. It was Prince Andrew's first visit since his release from jail, but the memory did not sour his enjoyment. Philip secured special leave from Gordonstoun to attend, and, it appears, seized the chance to impress, recounting 'tales of wild Scottish adventure' to his cousin Alexandra. But on the morning of the funeral he was less heroic. He felt ill due to the lobster he had eaten at dinner the night before. Resplendent in his first morning coat and silk top hat, he saw his father form the guard of honour with the Princes Nicholas, Christopher and Paul beside the triple bier; he watched the eight bishops assemble with solemn dignity; he listened to the music; then, in horror, he whispered agonizingly to Alexandra 'I'm going to be sick!'

Prince Philip somehow maintained control of himself throughout the ceremony but in the car, during the procession back to the palace, he vomited into his hat. How to dispose of the noxious object was now the problem and one which Philip resolved at the palace by thrusting it into the hands of a surprised aide.

This had been Philip's introduction to royal functions, an experience which, prompted by the pomp and pageantry, appears to have awakened curiosity in his Glücksburg ancestry. He asked many questions, probing the different relationships, for he was in the line of succession to the throne. Regrettably his most knowledgeable informant was not there; at that moment, Princess Alice was recuperating from a heart complaint in a Swiss nursing home.

It was with no regret that Philip, now sixteen, returned to Athens the following year. This second royal event – the wedding of the future King Paul I, then Crown Prince of Greece, to the vivacious Princess Frederika of Brunswick – was to be of significance to him. Prince Peter, King Michael and himself were chosen to be the three best men. Peter and Michael held the golden crowns over the heads of the bride and bridegroom as they exchanged vows and Philip merely looked dignified in an attendant role. But to his delight the ceremony united him with both his parents. Princess Alice, anxious to resume her charitable work, now lived quietly with an elderly companion, Madame Socopol, and a maid, in a house in Kolonaki Square in the centre of Athens. It has been suggested that there still lingered in the Princess's mind 'the haunting image of her favourite Aunt Ella'. Her mother's eldest sister had married the Grand Duke Serge of Russia. But when an assassin left her widowed, she had bestowed her worldly goods on the poor and founded Russia's sole sisterhood of nursing. Aunt Ella's philanthropy and religious devotion had stimulated reverence in others. For instance, Princess Louise, writing in her diary of a pre-war cruise on the Volga, had recorded: 'We stopped for Aunt Ella to go to church again. As she has now taken Holy Orders she naturally can hardly pass a town with a church without thinking she should go to a service.' This saintly life had been revered in Tsarist Russia but the Bolsheviks murdered her, brutally casting her down a disused mine-shaft. To her memory, a requiem is sung three times yearly at a Russian convent on the Mount of Olives.

To Princess Alice, Aunt Ella's ministrations to the poor both inspired and challenged. She had thus returned to Greece, mixing with the poor, and fostering her cottage industry specializing in Greek embroidery. Living so far away, the times when Prince Philip could visit his mother were obviously scant. Her niece, Alexandra, recalling a reunion between mother and son, wrote:

'I can see Aunt Alice continually glancing at the clock ... when Philip was expected. To welcome him on these comparatively infrequent occasions a large meal was always prepared ... I would find myself in the overcrowded rooms, crammed with old-fashioned furniture and well stocked with signed photographs of innumerable Battenbergs.... Aunt Alice has rarely abandoned the religious costume she has worn for many years. Long before she founded her own nursing order on the Isle of Tinos, she experimented with suitably austere costumes, oblivious of any quiet amusement she caused. Not that Aunt Alice lacked a sense of humour. At one time she liked to frequent a cinema that showed old classic silent films, chiefly for the joy of lip-reading ... These glimpses of real life from the movies were all the more comical for Aunt Alice's explosive method of blurting them out.'

Unwittingly, perhaps the wedding of Prince Paul was a cardinal turning-point in Prince Philip's life. Living together, though briefly, in the tranquillity of Princess Alice's home, the Princes Andrew and Philip seized the opportunity to discuss the future. Now that national affairs were more stable in Greece, the villa at Corfu again presented itself as a home. But as experience had taught, life in Greece could be both dangerous and unpredictable. However, at this time there was certain pressure to arrange Philip's enlistment at the Greek Nautical College, with the tempting hint that rapid progress in the Hellenic navy would be facilitated. Accounts differ as to who applied the pressure. Some attribute it to members of the Greek Royal Family; others that it was Prince Andrew himself. Or was it the pro-royalist element then in power in Greece? One cannot imagine that Prince Andrew, who never left Paris to reside at Mon Repos, made the suggestion. He had been disowned by Greece, and the rancour of banishment had never left him. Anyway, the outcome was that Prince Philip did not yield to enticement. Like his paternal grandfather, Prince Louis of Battenberg, he had chosen to lead the life of an Englishman.

Philip therefore returned to Gordonstoun for his final year – a period marred by two personal tragedies. Although Princess Marina solicitously telephoned him, hoping to assuage the grief, he had already learnt from Dr Hahn that his sister Cecile and her husband Prince George had died in an accident on their way to Britain. Flying in a fog, their plane had crashed into a factory chimney at Ostend, killing all on board. Philip had been anticipating a reunion at the wedding in London of Prince Louis of Hesse to the Hon. Margaret Campbell-Geddes, Lord Geddes's daughter. Others who died included the Grand Duchess Eleonore of Hesse-Darmstadt, the bridegroom's mother, and Prince Philip's two small nephews, Louis and Alexander of Hesse.

The second lamentable loss had even greater personal implications. Though only forty-six, the Marquess of Milford Haven, the person whom Philip had grown to accept as his foster father, died in the autumn of 1938 of cancer. It was yet another twist of fate in the Prince's life. At Prince Andrew's request, Lord Louis Mountbatten now acted *in loco parentis* for him. The benevolent Uncle George had been the kindly mentor in Prince Philip's childhood and adolescence; now Uncle Dickie would be the major influence in young manhood. George Milford Haven had justly earned his nephew's affection, but to Prince

Philip, Lord Mountbatten – an aristocrat of pulsating energy, a man of creative flair and quick decisions, the destroyer commander with panache – was his hero. Uncle George was someone to respect – even love; but Uncle Dickie was a man to emulate. Not until now, it has been claimed, had Louis shown any concern for his nephew's future other than a casual interest.

Whatever influences spurred Prince Philip to embark on a naval career, the close association with his sailor-uncle must have been a stimulant. It is generally accepted that Lord Mountbatten arranged for Philip to participate in the examinations for the Royal Naval College at Dartmouth as a special entry cadet from a public school. Meanwhile, there occurred what can be described as the 'Venetian Interlude'. Prince Philip visited Venice at the invitation of the widowed Princess Aspasia of Greece who, one writer has claimed, 'had ideas of a match' between Philip and her daughter Alexandra (who in her memoirs made no attempt to conceal her affection for her cousin). If that were so, Philip had no desire to be romantically entangled. Alexandra has since commented that Prince Philip's priorities were canals, gondolas, sailing, food and finally girls.

Now unaffected by the asceticism of Gordonstoun, he readily adapted himself to his new environment. In a sense he was displaying a Mountbatten trait – never shirking harsh conditions when times demanded but indulging the high social life whenever it presented itself. Alexandra revealed:

'I used to think that Gordonstoun had utterly exhausted him. He used to lie in bed until eleven or twelve o'clock, refusing every invitation to come out into the garden. Then he would come down demanding a full English-type breakfast of eggs and bacon from our Italian cook, which had to be done particularly as he wanted. Afterwards came lunch and then Philip was ready for every possible exploit. He was delighted to find that I had a speedboat and went off in it alone, leaving me stranded, for hours at a time.

'I exasperated him sometimes when I wanted to sit at home while he wanted to go out.... Couldn't he get a chair, I suggested, and finish *Busman's Holiday*, the book he was always talking about at the time. But Philip energetically wanted to be on the move.... Another evening Philip took command in a friend's sailing boat which he was convinced he could handle better than anybody else on board. This may have been the case on open water but not in the narrow twisting precincts of the Venice canals.... Venice, too, provided the occasion of probably the first and only time Philip ever got drunk. At Gordonstoun he had to promise abstinence from alcohol, so that at royal wedding parties he never more than sipped champagne. Released from this vow, I imagine Philip had to have one night out. Lord and Lady Melchett ... were giving a party at one of the fishermen's tavernas that had become fashionable at Torcello ... almost before we knew what was happening the Italian wine unexpectedly went to my cousin's head. He began to make us all laugh by dancing about the terrace like a young faun, a very handsome and graceful faun, I must admit. Then ... he began swinging from the pergola. Then it went beyond a joke, for the pergola collapsed, bringing the vine down with it, and Philip disappeared under the greenery. The enraged proprietor and his daughters – and a rueful, suddenly sobered Philip – cleaned up the mess. Happily, the Melchetts did not mind paying for the damage. I am sure they realized that a young man's intoxication on a Venetian evening was just as explosive as the chemicals from which their family fortune was founded.

Philip's father had been perturbed on hearing of the visit, and wrote: 'Philip still has to pass his exams. Whatever you do keep him out of girl trouble.' His son certainly did not lack invitations to parties and dances, or the companionship of blondes, brunettes and red-haired charmers. 'Philip gallantly and I think quite impartially squired them all,' but Alexandra recalled: 'He used to love having people in and they seemed to be quite different people each time. Then gradually one girl in the group began to stand out a little more than the others.' In the habit of borrowing Alexandra's motor-boat for his nocturnal cruising, Princess Aspasia allowed Philip to stay out a little longer on condition he did not stop the engine. Aunt Aspasia and Alexandra listened keenly as the launch chugged lazily across the lagoon. But eventually the phut-phut-phut of the motor suddenly stopped: 'There were five minutes of silence which we filled with surmise before we again heard the steady chug-chug-chug. Another loop or two were safely accomplished, and then again a few minutes' silence. The next day Philip sheepishly remarked: "We had trouble with the sparking plugs."'

Was this Philip's first affair of the heart or had Alexandra exaggerated the situation out of youthful jealousy? In later years she explained that 'there was talk that we might get engaged when we were older'. In that event Philip's life would have been channelled along a different course. But Philip seemed apathetic to Alexandra, who teased him about the bathing parties and picnics arranged for his pleasure. He in turn resented it and when he persisted in taking the same companion in Alexandra's boat while she herself stayed at home, 'we had a most uncousinly row'.

Some semblance of normality returned after David Milford Haven arrived to join in the Venetian frolics before Prince Philip returned to England to try and qualify for Dartmouth.

3

A Naval Prince Charming

During his last year at Gordonstoun, Prince Philip held the exalted rank of Guardian, or head boy. Moreover, he excelled as captain of the hockey and cricket teams. Briefly, his period at Gordonstoun had been fulfilled with distinction. In his final report Dr Hahn commented with prophetic insight:

'Prince Philip is universally trusted, liked and respected. He has the greatest sense of service of all the boys in the school. He is a born leader, but will need the exacting demands of a great service to do justice to himself. His best is outstanding; but his second best is not good enough. Prince Philip will make his mark in any profession but will have to prove himself in a full trial of strength.'

But in due course the results of the special entry examination at Dartmouth did not tally with Hahn's prediction. During the winter of 1938–9 Prince Philip went to Chelmsford for a cramming course, living-in with a Mr and Mrs Mercer, a naval coach and his wife, who were extremely impressed by his simplicity and modesty. The tutor discovered in Philip an amenable and courteous pupil and had no difficulty retaining his interest for study. Recreation amounted to little more than a visit to a cinema on a Saturday night or listening to gramophone records or the radio with the Mercers' daughter. The coach and his wife were somewhat surprised to note that pocket money was rather restricted.

Sitting for the examination in the spring, Prince Philip was the sixteenth among the thirty-four candidates who qualified. The placing did not appear to testify to Hahn's prophecy of rare leadership, but it should be explained that in the difficult oral examination Philip attained 380 marks out of a maximum of 400. The tests, in the main, had indicated that he was more endowed with self-reliance, intelligence and sound judgment – the basic ingredients of leadership. In fairness, too, Philip – who competed at the late age of eighteen – came from a public school whereas most of the other candidates were products of naval cadet centres. According to one writer, David Milford Haven attributed Philip's mediocre attainment to the interlude in Venice.

The date was 4 May 1939 when Prince Philip donned the uniform of a Royal Naval cadet. As throughout his school career, he quickly became the cynosure of the sports field. Highly competent on the squash court, by sheer merit he drew attention to himself in the Devonport Athletic Championships; his javelin throw put Dartmouth in the van of competitors. Cricket also claimed his enthusiasm. As for Lord Mountbatten, it has been contended that from now on he nurtured his nephew's progress, advising at every stage of his career. Certainly Uncle Dickie's own meteoric rise to naval distinction would be there for Philip to imitate, and indeed it is from this time one senses the Mountbatten influence really taking root. As if to demonstrate to his nephew what future standards he must attain, Lord Louis himself achieved first place in his own specific final course before embarking on wartime service. At Dartmouth Philip's star was soon seen to be in the ascendant, there receiving the King's Dirk as the leading cadet of his term and the Eardley–Howard–Crockett award as the best all-round cadet of his year. The exhilarating effects of British naval life, plus the excitement of the outbreak of war, now shattered all thoughts of transferring eventually to the Hellenic navy, if ever they really existed.

Years later Prince Philip could reflect on Dartmouth as a fateful cross-roads in his destiny, for it was there that a crucial incident in his life occurred; he really became aware of the Princess who, unknown to him then, was to be his future wife. Various claims are made as to when the paths of Prince Philip and Princess Elizabeth had previously crossed. It is recorded that the first occasion was at a family lunch given at Buckingham Palace by King George v and Queen Mary. Philip was then eleven and Elizabeth six. One authoritative writer, however, contends that the Princess never met her future Prince Charming until she was eight. There is the possibility that they were guests at Coppins, the home of Philip's cousin, Princess Marina, then married to the Duke of Kent, and they may have met occasionally at the Mountbatten penthouse. Both were present at the coronation of King George vi and Queen Elizabeth, but so far because of the disparity in ages there had been little impact.

Whatever the past, a certain date – 22 July 1939 – would be a fateful day, marking the most conspicuous point in a relationship which, if it really existed, had been haphazard. The King and Queen, accompanied by their daughters, visited Dartmouth. For George vi (then unaware of the eventual aftermath), there was a sense of nostalgia; for the first time he was returning to a boyhood haunt where, because of their royal status, both he and his elder brother David had been tormented at times by fellow cadets. What has been claimed to be of some portent (although one can find no justification for it) was the presence of Lord Mountbatten. For some while Uncle Dickie had been on Tyneside helping in the fitting out of the destroyer *Kelly*, but for the time being he was the King's naval ADC for the short cruise in the gold and white *Victoria and Albert*, the royal yacht. Dartmouth, it has been contended, gave scope to Lord Mountbatten's opportunist mind. Quite unexpectedly the programme had to be drastically changed when the King was informed that several cadets were sick with mumps. To avoid the danger of infection, the Queen ordered that Elizabeth and Margaret must not attend the church service or mix with the boys. Philip, at the instance of Lord Mountbatten, was therefore deputed to amuse his cousins. Assuming this to be correct (and one can find nothing in confirmation), this imputation that Lord Mountbatten manoeuvred to gain for his nephew his present exalted place is both baseless and unwarranted; it attributes powers which doubtless he has never possessed.

The royal party had already been conducted to the house of

the commandant, Captain (subsequently Admiral Sir Frederick) Dalrymple-Hamilton, and it was to the Captain's House that the lanky Prince, well groomed in summer 'whites', was summoned. To Miss Marion Crawford, the governess, Philip appeared as a 'fair-haired boy, rather like a Viking with a sharp face and piercing blue eyes'. Until boredom crept in, Philip entertained the Princesses with a model railway on the drawing-room floor. There were libations of lemonade and ginger biscuits, then Philip strolled with the young sisters through the college grounds. Elizabeth and Margaret, sheltered as yet in a royal backwater, were a striking contrast to the sophisticated and self-assured Prince. It appears that Miss Crawford was inclined to regard him as somewhat bumptious, and more so when he displayed his prowess by leaping energetically over a tennis net. But the thirteen-year-old Elizabeth is credited with the remark: 'How good he is, Crawfie! How high he can jump!'

That day George VI invited the officers and captain-cadets aboard the royal yacht. Although Prince Philip was a mere cadet it was arranged that he should also attend, and he was invited for lunch – at Elizabeth's specific request, so it is claimed – the following day. This would be the last time that Elizabeth and Philip would see each other for almost six years.

After the Royal Family and the *Victoria and Albert* moved out into Dart Bay, many of the cadets manned boats and loyally followed the royal yacht until the King told Captain Sir Dudley North: 'This is ridiculous and quite unsafe. You must signal them to go back.' Gradually the boats turned – all save one. Philip carried on heedless of the King's apprehension and disfavour. 'The young fool,' fumed King George. 'He must go back otherwise we will have to heave to and send him back.' Philip dutifully turned back for the shore.

Some writers have naïvely and foolishly allowed their imaginations to build the Dartmouth incident into a romance. This was not the case, and to write that Philip 'standing up (in the boat) in a final gesture received the most gracious and tender acknowledgment from the young Princess' is both nauseating and hyperbole. It is more likely that Prince Philip was giving free reign to his extrovert nature, although it has since been suggested that it was an expression of his respect for the King. The real significance of that July event is that, as far as one can assess, it appears to be the first authentic meeting between Princess Elizabeth and Prince Philip – and, as they themselves have since revealed, certainly the first that they themselves can remember. From this time onward, there would be sporadic correspondence which would endure the vicissitudes of war.

With the outbreak of hostilities it was manifest to the older cadets at Dartmouth that within months they would join the fleet as midshipmen. Apparently Uncle Dickie impressed upon Philip at the outset that he must pass out well. Philip set about the task with such gusto that, to some of his class-mates, it bordered on over-bearing aggressiveness. Probably an element of the German arrogance mingled with extreme ambition and the intolerance to which Dr Hahn had drawn attention. But the desire to excel could also have been misconstrued. However, any trace of haughtiness would be allayed when subsequently he mixed with all ranks at sea. Luckily his innate humour was a match for any conceit. The fact is that Philip applied himself with tenacity and was judged to be well ahead of his fellows in seamanship. Where necessary, determined plodding coped with the more normal studies. With the Eardley–Howard–Crockett award went a book token valued at £2. It was in character – certainly in keeping with his mood at this period – that he chose a book on strategy, *The Defence of Britain*, by Captain Liddell Hart.

The date, 1 January 1940, was a momentous one for Prince Philip; he was posted as a midshipman to the old battleship *Ramillies* which, stationed at Colombo, escorted transports of the Australian contingent to the Mediterranean. To an imaginative youth naval life had begun as a great adventure, as well as satisfying an urge to travel. Because of his insatiable energy and curiosity, when *Ramillies* berthed at Australian ports he shunned the social round, preferring action on a cattle station and life with the jackaroos. Philip served in *Ramillies* for four months. It was a safe but – according to himself – an unsatisfactory posting, for he wanted to experience the heat and excitement of war. But until circumstances changed, this would be debarred simply because he was a foreign prince. On Lord Mountbatten's advice, Philip had applied for British citizenship, only to find that all naturalization had been suspended for the rest of the war. And while Greece and Turkey escaped Nazi conquest, Prince Philip must be classified as a neutral citizen. In London both the Lords of the Admiralty and the Foreign Office shuddered at the embarrassment that would result if Philip was killed or taken prisoner by the Germans.

Yet another problem for Prince Philip had been his title. At the Admiralty their Lordships had issued an order instructing all – regardless of rank – to address him as a prince, a dictate which, because of his age and modest officer status, Philip heartily disliked. He resolved an awkward situation through his own initiative. When asked his name he merely answered 'Philip' and that became the general acceptance.

Prince Philip was now transferred to the complement of HMS *Kent* and later to HMS *Shropshire* at Durban – two rather antiquated light cruisers of the County Class suitable only for convoy work. As his own personal accounts describe, the change of ships did not ease the sense of inactivity. Like all midshipmen, it was compulsory for Prince Philip to keep a log – 'to record in their own hand all matters of interest or importance in the work that is carried out, on their stations, in their Fleet, or in their ship. The objects of keeping the Journal are to train Midshipmen in (a) the power of observation, (b) the power of expression, (c) the habit of orderliness.' The log had to be kept during the whole of a midshipman's time at sea. Produced now and again for inspection by the captain or other superior, it was a significant item 'at the examination in Seamanship for the rank of Lieutenant'. A bound volume with marbled end-papers, the log to some extent mirrored the mind and character of the person who made the entries. Such items as sketches of ports and ships' equipment, maps and plans of anchorages, and charts of courses steered were expected to adorn the log. In Philip's case his penchant for art caused him to be liberal and precise in technical detail in his illustrations, often resorting to multi-colour.

Of this period, one extract from Prince Philip's log explains: 'A few minutes after nine o'clock, on Sunday, October 1st 1940, I walked aboard His Majesty's Ship *Shropshire*, the third ship in eight months to receive this singular honour.' Philip was joking, but one senses an element of frustration, a high-spirited young man irked by what in effect was a pacifist role. But life had not been entirely irksome. To satisfy his unquenchable curiosity and to counter restlessness during shore leave in Colombo, he had inspected a tea plantation, witnessed the festival of Pera-Hera at Kandy, engaged in a mine-sweeper patrol, and personally operated the commander-in-chief's barge – a 40-foot power-boat, with twin engines, screws and rudders – 'and about the only thing one could not make it do was spread wings and fly off'.

In his book on the Asia Minor campaign, Prince Andrew had evinced himself as a writer of some skill and cogency. As a midshipman his son displayed keen powers of observation, writing in a simple style in highly legible writing. For instance, of the festival at Kandy, he wrote:

'I counted eighty elephants in one of these processions all beautifully dressed with bright coloured sheets embroidered with silver and brass. All the old Kandy chiefs took part in those processions and they too were wonderful to look at. Four-cornered gold crowns on their heads then short beautifully embroidered jackets of purple velvet or silver and gold brocade. Then thirty yards of very fine white silk edged with gold, wound round their middles which made them look as if they had enormous stomachs. They had close fitting trousers on with pointed red leather shoes on their feet. Each of these chiefs was preceded by his dancers.'

At first there had been some reaction to Prince Philip in *Kent*, the flagship of the China station. After a two-and-a-half-year commission, war had deprived the ship's company of much needed leave. To the irritation of the ranks, regulations were strictly observed – 'matchstick sentries, a change of rig five or six times a day, and an Admiral on the quarterdeck', observed a rating. Now, being compelled to contend as well with a member of the Royal House of Greece was carrying matters too far. But the fear that Philip might allow his aura of royalty to disrupt was unfounded. He rolled and smoked cigarettes with the ratings and ran 'all over the ship trying to obey instructions from a host of gold braid, smiling and cheerful to everyone, no matter what their rank'. Thus he endeared himself, and when the captain expressed a desire for fresh fish, Philip helped 'to blow them up with small charges. We let go about four charges and collected about fifty or sixty fish. Four of us got into bathing suits and as the fish came to the surface we dived in and threw them into the boat. Eventually after a most interesting day we returned aboard at 1800.' *Kent* was anchored at the time off Chagos Island in the Solomons.

Of all the places visited at this time, the fledgling officer wrote that the 'grand unselfish hospitality with which we were welcomed by the people of Durban will live in our memories for years to come'. But even here the glitter could be tarnished. Describing one specific incident, Prince Philip explained:

'We soon discovered that the person responsible for our late leave being all night was not as humane as we thought. There was field-training for all midshipmen on the wharf from quarter past nine to quarter to twelve. The fact that one feels rather weak at that time after a run ashore on the previous evening, and that the temperature in the shade hovered around 80°F., and that the gunner's mate was also recovering and anyhow displeased by our efforts to manipulate an oily rifle in a military manner, did not help the rebirth of the "joy-of-living" which had ebbed away during the spell in the Red Sea, and was only just becoming apparent again.'

Until there were more dramatic events to record, Prince Philip's log inevitably contained a degree of trivia. For the moment he would occupy himself with minor matters, but always there is that acute sense of precise detail. He had grown attached to *Ramillies*, for instance, but disliked the prickly heat: 'Nobody ever turns in. The most popular sleeping quarters are in the gun room, where the midshipmen sleep in two armchairs, two sofas and on the table. It gets very hot at night, since the ship is darkened and every scuttle is shut with deadlights.' For that reason alone he was pleased to transfer to *Kent*: 'The ventilation is so much better that it is quite possible to sleep below decks in comfort. There is no danger whatsoever of hitting one's head on the deckhead or beams.'

The naval action for which Prince Philip yearned drew close. On 9 April 1940 Denmark was invaded by the Nazis. Although his ancestral background on the paternal side was essentially Danish, and despite the fact that he had been issued with a Danish passport, Philip himself had been born a Prince of Greece. Therefore it was debatable at that time as to what his true nationality was in a legal sense. But on 28 October Italy – Germany's axis partner – invaded Greece. Philip could no longer be classified as a neutral; the country of his birth was unmistakably dragged into the global struggle. Then serving in South Africa, Prince Philip wrote to the First Sea Lord, Admiral Sir Dudley Pound, requesting to be posted to a theatre of war. Opinions vary on whether Lord Mountbatten exercised some influence or not. The fact is that early in January 1941 Prince Philip was transferred to *Valiant* of the Mediterranean Fleet.

Of the Queen Elizabeth Class, *Valiant* had been a veteran of the First World War but was still formidable, with eight huge 15-inch guns and fourteen 6-inch guns as well as the nucleus of anti-aircraft armament. A few days after Prince Philip joined his ship, she participated in the bombardment of Bardia for the opening of Wavell's first advance into Cyrenaica. Midshipman Prince Philip had been assigned part of the command of *Valiant*'s searchlight control and from this vantage point it was exciting to see the great guns in action. In his own words: 'That evening at dusk the Battle Fleet put to sea and shortly afterwards we were told we were going to bombard Bardia on the Libyan coast. We arrived ... on Thursday morning at dawn. In the dark the flashes of the guns could be seen a long way out to sea. We went to action stations at 0730, and at 0810 the bombardment commenced ... The whole operation was a very spectacular affair.' This was action more in keeping with Prince Philip's temperament. A few days later drama reached greater intensity off the south of Sicily:

'At dawn action stations on Friday gun flashes were sighted on the starboard bow. We increased speed to investigate, and by the time we were within five miles it was almost daylight. *Bonaventure* signalled that *Southampton* and herself were engaging two enemy destroyers. We could just see one of these destroyers blowing up in a cloud of smoke and spray. The other escaped. Shortly after this the destroyer *Gallant* hit a mine and her bow was blown off, and floated slowly away on the swell. ... At noon two torpedo bombers attacked us, but a quick alteration of course foiled their attempt, and their fish passed down the port side. Shortly after this sixteen German dive-bombers attacked the *Illustrious*. She was hit aft and amidships and fires broke out. Then the bombers concentrated on us and five bombs dropped fairly close.'

For some while Greece had endured the anxieties of an uneasy peace. Fearing invasion the Greeks had agreed that should Italy attack, Britain could establish a garrison in Crete, with coastal defence guns and air base. From the time Mussolini seized Albania, the Greeks had feared an Italian attack, for they alone formed the obstacle to Italian imperial designs in the eastern Mediterranean. General Metaxas, the little Greek dictator, strove to avoid conflict with either Mussolini or Hitler. Superficially the old city of Athens was prosperous and noisy but behind the chatter in the cafés there was a restless undercurrent of fear.

This troubled atmosphere had prevailed when Prince Philip arrived to spend three months' leave with his mother during the summer of 1940. Some years had elapsed since Princess Alice, who had settled once more in Athens, had last seen her son. It had required all her fortitude to overcome her grief on hearing of the death in November 1937 of her daughter Cecile, but as Meriel Buchanan, her intimate friend revealed – 'some inner spiritual force seemed to give her back her strength and restore her serenity, her composure and her resignation'. In Greece Princess Alice had turned to charitable works and out of them had emerged the desire to create a modest religious community. Perhaps the inspiration came from the memory of her mother's eldest sister, Aunt Ella. But unlike her devout ancestor Princess Alice, devoid of wealth, could erect neither church nor hospital. Moreover, the Greek Orthodox Church was apathetic towards her cause. For a while her ardour was in no way compensated. The simple grey home-made habit which she herself had designed hung rather forlornly in a wardrobe at Tatoi, until gradually she wore it in public. Finally she had resolved to found a children's orphanage, and for the purpose her brother-in-law, Prince George of Greece, granted her facilities at his house in Athens. The accommodation was quite spacious, the reception rooms being adapted into nurseries and clinics. The bedrooms still retained their normal use but now as dormitories. There were many difficulties to resolve when Philip was there, but what concerned him most was the plight his mother might encounter if Greece was overrun.

That was paramount in his mind when he rejoined his ship. Princess Alice herself, resolute and strong-minded, was fatalistic like most of the Athenians, even when Italian troops concentrated in the autumn beyond the Albanian frontier. When the blow fell it came treacherously and completely as a surprise.

On the evening of 27 October, stragglers in Athens' Kifissia Road curiously watched the guests arrive at the Italian Embassy where Count Grazzi, the Italian Minister, was host at a banquet celebrating the anniversary of the Fascist march on Rome. Perhaps General Metaxas, adorned with medals and orders, derived some scrap of relief on hearing Grazzi's toast: 'Long live the friendship between Italy and Greece.' It appeared that Greece had been reprieved – temporarily at least. Listening to Grazzi's reassuring words of detente, even the most cynical might have been excused for sleeping more contentedly in their beds that night. Yet at 3 a.m. Joannis Metaxas was

awakened by the shrill ringing of his telephone. 'This is the
French ambassador. I must see you immediately, Excellency,'
came a voice. Though rather evasive, Metaxas replied: 'Very
well, come along to the house. I shall be waiting.' To his
astonishment Metaxas opened the front door not to the French
ambassador but to Count Grazzi. In the study the Italian
opened his case, handed Metaxas some type-written papers,
then waited in silence. Italy, Metaxas read, required the use of
strategic bases and free passage for her troops – 'as a guarantee
of Greece's neutrality. The Italian Government demands that
Greece shall not oppose this occupation ... Its troops do not
come as an enemy of the Greek people.' Count Grazzi informed
that his government's ultimatum expired at six that morning.
'You will allow these facilities, Excellency. For Greece it would
be ...' 'No,' barked Metaxas. 'You can tell them no.'

The next day King George II of the Hellenes told the nation
that Greece was at war, fighting for her integrity and independence. In Italy, boarding the last diplomatic train, Philip's
cousin Alexandra and her mother accompanied members of
the Greek Embassy across Yugoslavia to Athens. As the war
intensified and Mussolini's bombers harassed the capital, the
Royal Family took refuge in a shelter built in the cellars of the
Old Palace. But when they grew accustomed to the raids they
often gathered on the roof-garden. Sometimes Princess Alice
would be the last to reach the Palace's relative safety, stopping
on the way to round up children in the streets.

To her surprise and joy, she was unexpectedly joined by her
son; *Valiant* had called at Piraeus and Prince Philip had been
granted leave. Naturally he spent it with his relations who,
defying the bombs, arranged parties and dances in their homes.
During one night raid Philip was accused of exhibitionism by
making 'knowledgeable comments', but Princess Alexandra, to
whom Philip was 'gay, debonair, confident', wrote that he
'never talked naval shop and never had a word to say on his
personal naval duties. He would accept a dinner invitation, saying "Maybe I can come", and this was the only assurance
we had.'

Sir Henry Channon attended one of these events. He noted in

his diary that on 21 January 1941 he was invited to 'an enjoyable Greek cocktail party. Philip of Greece was there. He is
extraordinarily handsome, and I recalled my afternoon's conversation with Princess Nicholas. He is to be our Prince Consort,
and that is why he is serving in our Navy.' Commenting on this
entry years after his marriage, Prince Philip remarked that presumably it had been mentioned that he was eligible and the
sort of person Princess Elizabeth might marry – 'People had
only to say that for somebody like Chips Channon to go one
step further and say it is already decided.'

Behind the façade of gaiety, there lurked fears for the future.
Although one could laud the heroic defiance of the Greeks,
obviously once the German mechanized columns roared into
Greece the members of the Royal Family must flee. Prince
Philip, it is said, tried to extract a promise from his mother to
leave with the rest of the Royal Family, but characteristically
she merely replied: 'We will see.' As in the First World War,
Princess Alice saw the Greek Royal Family torn apart by conflicting loyalties. But this time it was even more pronounced
and had split her own immediate domestic world. Her son
Prince Philip, like her brother Lord Louis Mountbatten, wore
the uniform of Britain's Royal Navy while her sons-in-law were
high-ranking German officers. It was a sad and confused situation arising from the quirks of war. But of more immediate concern was the manner in which the Nazis would react if Princess
Alice elected to stay in Greece. Whatever the outcome, when
the day came she calmly but stubbornly declined to leave
Athens. At least, she reasoned, she could now communicate
with her daughters when the Germans overran Greece. For
news of other members of her family Princess Alice depended
on the occasional letter from a Swedish source. There was profound concern for her husband, but in time she learnt from her
sister Louise in neutral Sweden that Prince Andrew now lived
in the south of France. 'He still lives on board the yacht *Davida*
at Cannes,' she wrote, 'and says he is not hungry as he is a
small eater. Food conditions are near starving on the Riviera.
But he is now cut off from outside news ... the port authorities
have confiscated his radio.' It would be through his Aunt

Louise Mountbatten, wife of the Swedish Crown Prince, that Philip would also glean infrequent messages concerning his parents and three sisters.

Now that she had completely isolated herself from her relations, Princess Alice occupied her days nursing and attending to the needs of the poor. Although in the initial stages the Nazis did not ignore her, they did not molest her. Neither did they try to use her as a political pawn. For a while guards were placed outside her quarters until it was finally appreciated that they could be better employed elsewhere. As well as working in the crowded hospitals, Princess Alice now held herself responsible for safeguarding twenty orphaned children left parentless by war. But her altruism was harassed by conditions which were virtually untenable. The miseries mounted under the Nazis. Rations, which had always been meagre, now dwindled to almost non-existence. It was a period of strain during which Princess Alice revealed the depth of her character and independence. When a hospital colleague tacitly arranged for her to receive extra supplies of Red Cross food, she adamantly refused to sign for anything beyond the normal allowance. Anxious over her welfare, this same friend bought Alice some bare necessities on the black market, taking care to conceal the source from which they came.

The horrors of guerrilla fighting intensified the wretchedness of war-torn Athens, reaching a climax when gas, electricity and water were abruptly cut off. Sometimes when searching for food for her hungry orphans, Princess Alice would return through the streets, her bag empty, risking death from a sniper's bullet. Not until the British were back on Greek soil in 1944, and Mr Harold Macmillan, the future British Prime Minister, visited her from Cairo, was the outside world conscious of her plight. Mr Macmillan's account implies that Princess Alice was living in 'humble, not to say somewhat squalid conditions ... she made very little complaint, but when I pressed her to know if there was anything we could do, she admitted that she and her old lady-in-waiting needed food. They had bread but no stores of any kind – no sugar, tea, coffee, rice or tinned foods.' Army supplies were quickly provided under an arrangement made by

Mr Macmillan, but most of these went to others whom Princess
Alice considered were in greater need.

That year brightened with the glimmering of Allied victory,
but ended tragically for Princess Alice. Prince Andrew died.
Only the occasional filtering through of news had acquainted
him of the fate of his family. As for himself, for years he had been
aware of the heart complaint that finally destroyed him. Death,
however, did not overtake him before he experienced the joy
and excitement of liberation – the Allied landing in southern
France. A little before daybreak on 3 December 1944, in a villa
that friends had lent to him in Monte Carlo, he rose from his
bed, put on his dressing-gown then sat in an armchair and died.
Prince Andrew was buried with all the honours that the small
principality of Monaco could bestow on him. He was conveyed
to the Russian Orthodox Church in Nice where units of the
French army participated in the ritual of burial. Like so many
then residing on the Riviera, Prince Andrew had lived – and
now died – on credit. His funeral expenses were defrayed by
the Greek Consul-General.

To revert to the day in 1941 when Prince Philip's leave expired,
he returned to *Valiant* and the sobering experience of his first
naval action. The Battle of Cape Matapan would drastically
change the balance of naval power in the Mediterranean. The
dash of Admiral Sir Andrew Cunningham across the Mediterranean, the delaying tactics of carrier-borne Swordfish and
Greece-based planes dive-bombing through anti-aircraft fire,
and the relentless chase in the darkness, were the salient factors
that resulted in success. But the most lethal action of all was
the night encounter by the British battle squadron with an
Italian fleet. In noisy, exciting minutes the battleships *Valiant*,
Warspite and *Barham* blasted to total destruction three of
Italy's heavy cruisers and two destroyers and the battleship
Vittorio Veneto and other warships were seriously harmed.
Fleet tactical orders allotted to *Valiant* the duty of illuminating
enemy targets. Returning south-eastwards, presumably attempt-
ing to help the crippled cruiser *Pola*, the presence of the Italian
fleet was betrayed by radar. The enemy ships were first lit up

by the destroyer *Greyhound*, but in an instant *Valiant*'s blinding lights picked out the targets, trapping them like moths in a flame. Commanding a section of *Valiant*'s searchlight control in this swift and lively engagement was Midshipman Prince Philip. Accurate illumination of the Italian fleet was vital for the gunnery. The fact that three quarters of *Valiant*'s 30-odd rounds were direct hits testifies to that accuracy.

Admiral Cunningham mentioned Philip in the subsequent despatches, but Rear-Admiral Sir Charles Morgan felt inspired to write: 'Thanks to his (Philip's) alertness and appreciation of the situation, we were able to sink in five minutes two eight-inch-gun Italian cruisers.' Prince Philip's significance here is somewhat exaggerated. One cannot believe that, but for the presence of the royal midshipman, the Navy would have been thwarted in their efforts to sink units of the Italian fleet. To commemorate his baptism of fire Prince Philip's cousin, the King of Greece, awarded him the Greek War Cross for valour.

For a description of this action one prefers to quote Philip's more modest account. He explained that

'if any ship illuminated a target I was to switch on and illuminate it for the rest of the fleet, so when this ship was lit up by a rather dim light from what I thought was the flagship I switched on our midship light which picked out the enemy cruiser and lit her up as if it were broad daylight. She was only seen complete in the light for a few seconds as the flagship had already opened fire, and as her first broadside landed and hit she was blotted out from just abaft the bridge to right astern. We fired our first broadside about 7 seconds after the flagship with very much the same effect. The broadside only consisted of "A" and "B" turrets as the after turret would not bear. By now all the secondary armament of both ships had opened fire and the noise was considerable. The Captain and the Gunnery Officer now began shouting from the bridge for the searchlights to train left. The idea that there might have been another ship, with the one we were firing at, never entered my head, so it was some few moments before I was persuaded to relinquish the blazing target and search for another one I had no reason to believe was there. However, training to the left, the light picked up another cruiser, ahead of the first one by some three or four cables. As the enemy was so close the light did not illuminate the whole ship but only about three-quarters of it, so I trained left over the whole ship until the bridge structure was in the centre of the beam. The effect was rather like flashing a strong torch on a small model about 5 yards away ... She was illuminated in an undamaged condition for the period of about 5 seconds when our second broadside left the ship, and almost at once she was blotted out from stern to stern ...

'When that broadside was fired, owing to the noise of the secondary armament, I did not hear the "ting-ting" from the DCT. The result was that the glasses were rammed into my eyes, the flash almost blinding me. Luckily the searchlight was not affected, so that when I was able to see something again the light was still on target. Four more broadsides were fired at the enemy, and more than 7% of the shells must have hit. The only correction given by the control officer was "left 1°", as he thought we were hitting a bit far aft. When the enemy had completely vanished in clouds of smoke and steam we ceased firing and switched the light off.'

Some time later Prince Philip said that the incident 'was as near murder as anything could be in wartime. The cruisers just burst into tremendous sheets of flame.'

Meanwhile, the British War Cabinet opined that the King of the Hellenes and his government should leave the Greek mainland and set up a national government in Crete. By so doing, they claimed, King George could escape from being made into an instrument of the Nazis. The King and M. Tsouderos, his new Prime Minister, concurred; George II insisting that for the sake of Greek morale and for the conduct of future Greek operations against the Germans, both he and the Royal Hellenic Government should stay on Greek soil as long as possible. On the morning of 26 April, the day before a German motor-cycle battalion entered Athens, the royal party – including leading members of the government – climbed aboard a flying boat to

escape to Crete. But as the aircraft was about to take off, the
King, Crown Prince Paul, and Colonel Levidis, the King's
Chamberlain, climbed out into the motor-boat alongside; King
George, on the spur of the moment, refused to abandon his
people until the final hour. Fears filled the Crown Princess
Frederika as she saw her husband return across the water to
the doomed capital that was already at the mercy of Goering's
planes. It was with relief that she welcomed him the following
day after the royal brothers and Levidis arrived in Crete at
Suda Bay.

The island of Crete in 1941 was indefensible. In a frantic but
belated attempt to bolster defences, Allied troops were conveyed to Crete. In *Valiant* Prince Philip witnessed these des-
perate measures, but action had come too late. When the
Battle of Crete erupted the Nazis would smash resistance within a week. In this futile situation most of the Greek party flew
on to Alexandria, but King George remained until he reluctantly fled in the destroyer *Decoy*.

Valiant did not, as is generally believed, escort *Decoy* to
Alexandria. Prince Philip, therefore, did not accompany his
kinsman. Instead, collaborating with destroyer and cruiser
squadrons, *Valiant* strove during the horrors of the Battle of
Crete to prevent German airborne landings. Typically, in his
description of the struggle on the third day of the battle (22
May) there is no exciting drama, but merely the basic facts.
He wrote:

'Next day things began to get worse. *Juno* was sunk. *Naiad*
_ and *Carlisle* were hit. A signal came asking for assistance, so
we turned and steamed at 20 knots ... As we came in sight
of the straits we saw *Naiad* and *Carlisle* being attacked by
bombers. We went right in to within ten miles of Crete and
then the bombing started in earnest. Stukas came over but
avoided the big ships and went for the crippled cruisers and
destroyer screens. *Greyhound* was hit right aft by a large
bomb, her stern blew up and she sank about twenty minutes
later. *Gloucester* and *Fiji* were sent in to help them ... Three
Me. 109s attacked *Warspite* as dive-bombers, and she was hit

just where her starboard forrard mounting was ... When we had got about 15 miles from the land 16 Stukas came out and attacked the two cruisers. *Gloucester* was badly hit and sank some hours later. The fleet then had some more attention, and we were bombed from a high level by a large number of small bombs dropped in sticks of twelve or more. One Dornier came straight for us from the port beam and dropped twelve bombs when he was almost overhead. We turned to port and ceased firing, when suddenly the bombs came whistling down, landing very close all down the port side.'

Valiant had been struck twice on the quarterdeck. 'One bomb exploded just abaft the quarterdeck screen on the port side ... The other landed within twenty feet of it, just inboard of the guard-rails, blowing a hole into the wardroom laundry ... There were only four casualties.'

While *Valiant* was being refitted at Alexandria, Prince Philip witnessed the shuttle service as ships desperately tried to rescue Allied troops from the débâcle in Crete. Some naval vessels would never return. *Calcutta* had been sunk and *Kashmir*, *Fiji*, *Greyhound* and *Gloucester* had gone down. Perhaps more significant to Philip was the loss of Lord Mountbatten's *Kelly*. His oil-smeared uncle was aboard *Kipling* which, while rescuing survivors, steamed over the submerged *Kelly* and 'slit a hole in three compartments forrard'. To his annoyance Lord Louis lost a dressing-case of gold-backed brushes as *Kelly*, struck by a thousand-pound bomb, turned turtle. Battle scarred, *Kandahar* arrived with David Milford Haven on board.

Thus a happy family reunion during shore leave had an ameliorating effect after the tragedies of war. Philip, David and Alexandra met again for the first time since their rendezvous in Venice.

'Now we were all three together again ready to do the town [she wrote]. We went out to a swimming-pool or beach and splashed happily in the sun. Philip had contrived to get hold of an absurdly small car which streaked through the streets with the noise of a thousand demons ... I liked David's lazy smile and I liked Philip's broad grin. At all events I was distressed at leaving them behind when we were ordered to move to the comparative safety of Cairo.

'But Philip soon tracked us to Shepheard's Hotel. In his little wasp of a car we went out to the Ghezira Club, swam or just talked through the long lazy afternoons when he was off duty. We ... went to Groppi's for tea. Philip used to talk even at this time of a home of his own, a country house in England he had planned to the last detail of fitments and furniture. This is so like Philip; once he has made up his mind on anything he always knows precisely where he is going, determined to make every plan come true.'

The only thing which marred those pleasant hours in Cairo were thoughts of Princess Alice, but having two sons-in-law who were senior German officers, Philip believed that the enemy would leave her undisturbed.

Due for promotion, Prince Philip, with four other midshipmen, was sent back to England during June, boarding at Port Said a Canadian Pacific liner, *Duchess of Atholl*, which was now used as a troopship. To avoid harassment and possible destruction by the Luftwaffe in the western Mediterranean, the ship took a devious route through the Red Sea to the Cape of Good Hope. For Philip there was compensation. King George II and his family had been installed at Groote Schuur, the home of General Smuts near Cape Town, and in company with Crown Princess Frederika he explored by car much of Cape Province.

At their own request Philip and his fellow midshipmen left South Africa in a different ship, their action being prompted by the disquieting sounds which had emanated from the engine-room of the *Duchess of Atholl* and the tiresome conditions caused by overcrowding. Then on its way to Canada to take on troops for Europe, the second ship was virtually empty. But before they reached Halifax in Nova Scotia they would regret the transfer. When the ship put in at Puerto Rico, the Chinese stokers deserted the ship, leaving the five midshipmen to be assigned as 'volunteers' to feed the boilers until their arrival at Newport News. Heaving coal into the furnaces of *Dreadnought* at Smyrna had been the youthful experience of Prince Louis of Battenberg. Now his grandson, clad in dirty shorts, his be- grimed body glistening with sweat, laboured in the scorching heat as the furnace doors clanged open. For his impromptu duties, Philip received a trimmer's certificate on reaching England.

Prince Philip later resented changing ships. Although he rented a car at Newport and hurriedly drove to Washington and back, this was a trifling experience compared with what might have been; her engines having broken down completely, the *Duchess of Atholl* remained in New York for three weeks for repairs.

Returning to London and its bombs and blackout, Prince Philip entered into the pleasures of social life. He frequented such places as the 400 Club and the Savoy Hotel, the haunts of officers on leave and the society set who danced and dined throughout the winter of 1941 oblivious, it seemed, to the cala- mity of the Far East. It was during this period – the winter of 1941–2 – that Philip was invited by King George VI to Bucking- ham Palace. Already he was famíliar with the homes of certain members of the Royal Family, notably Coppins, the Iver resi- dence of Princess Marina and the Duke of Kent.

The first time that he was presented to Queen Mary at Marl- borough House is somewhat vague. Aunt Nada, the widow of Uncle George Milford Haven, is reputed as having introduced her nephew, but this is of little account. Of greater interest is the knowledge that the Prince quickly won the goodwill of the elderly Queen. To Lady Airlie, her close friend, she described Prince Philip as 'intelligent ... plenty of common sense' and 'very handsome', with the attractive appearance of both the Glücksburgs and the Mountbattens. In short, Queen Mary arrived at the swift conclusion that Philip of Greece was a 'very bright and agreeable young man', and this rapport resulted in other visits. One writer asserts that it was not merely Philip's arresting personality that attracted, but also his skill at recounting risqué stories that normally circulated in an officers' mess. Somewhat incongruously, Queen Mary, at times censorious of the antics of young people, and whom the nation at large accepted as a paragon of etiquette and regal stateliness, was curiously addicted to the unexpurgated tale. It is well known that General Sir Arthur Slogett, formerly Director-General of the Royal Medical Corps in the First World War, who became her consultant physician and faithful confidant, regaled her with piquant stories and thus earned the nickname at Court of 'Naughty Arthur'.

Prince Philip could resume and strengthen associations in London because for the next two years he saw duty on home stations. For achieving four Firsts and a Second in his examinations, in February 1942 he was promoted sub-lieutenant with nine months' seniority out of a possible ten. He returned to sea in *Wallace*, the flotilla leader of the destroyers operating on east coast convoy duties from Rosyth to Sheerness – the hazardous 'E-boat Alley', with its bombs and torpedoes. Promoted lieutenant in July, at his captain's request he was appointed first lieutenant in the following October. Now twenty-one, he was the Royal Navy's youngest in this rank to become the senior executive officer in a vessel of that size. That was not enough; Philip insisted that the service routine, discipline and physical fitness of *Wallace*'s complement had to be unequalled in the squadron. However, an ebullient and humorous lieutenant in *Lauderdale*, Lieutenant Michael Parker, who had transferred from the Australian to the Royal Navy in 1938, entertained similar aspirations. Out of this rivalry would be born a close friendship. Indeed, after their marriage Parker, by then a lieutenant-commander, would be appointed equerry to both Princess Elizabeth and Prince Philip. When the Princess succeeded her father King George VI, Parker would work solely for Prince Philip.

In July 1943 *Wallace* left Scapa Flow for the Mediterranean, collaborating in the Allied invasion of Sicily. Though there were horrifying incidents both from the land and the air, this time there was not the forlorn sense of defeat experienced at Crete. *Wallace*, by naval standards, was an ancient ship. More-

over, she was in dire need of an overhaul, and after landing
Canadian troops she was withdrawn in September for a refit.

Back in Britain Philip stayed for eight months on home
stations. It was a period which would have much significance.

As a correspondent, Philip had the reputation of being
erratic, yet since 1940 he had maintained reasonable correspondence with Princess Elizabeth. There is nothing to imply
that at first Philip was anything but casually interested in the
child princess. As for Princess Elizabeth, no one has yet produced evidence that, at this period, her sentiments were anything more than extreme admiration. Shielded as she was,
rather remote from male friendship, she was doubtless impressed by her enchanting third cousin. The relationship would
begin to change after the Christmas festivities at Windsor
Castle.

During the war Princess Elizabeth and her sister Margaret
lived mostly at Windsor Castle in the thick-walled Lancaster
Tower with its winding staircase built in the reign of Henry VII.
Two years earlier, to raise funds for charity, the two Princesses
had written and produced the first of what would become an
annual pantomime held in Windsor's Waterloo Chamber. Here,
many years earlier, Queen Victoria had built a stage for household theatricals and for the occasions when she commanded
London companies to appear for her amusement. She would
ring a little gold bell to request the performance to begin.

Victoria would never know that by appearing on this self-
same stage her great-great-granddaughter would meet her true
Prince Charming. Invited to spend Christmas at Windsor with
the Royal Family, Prince Philip sat with the King and Queen
during a performance of *Aladdin*. Elizabeth was now seventeen, and the Principal Boy – and not only was there a gleam
from Aladdin's lamp. Elizabeth's governess, Miss Crawford,
wrote: 'There was a sparkle about her none of us had ever
seen before.'

Only nine people were present for dinner on Christmas
Eve. The King and Queen, Princess Elizabeth and Princess
Margaret, Prince Philip and four more guests. Philip chatted
with King George describing his experiences in *Wallace* at

Sicily, then the party retired to the drawing-room, turned out the lights and in the glow of firelight listened to ghost stories. Princess Margaret was not amused. 'We settled ourselves to be frightened,' she wrote, 'and we were *not*. Most disappointing.' But there was greater animation on the remaining evenings. The young people danced to a gramophone, and on the final night the little group was augmented by the staff and officers in charge of the Bofors guns protecting Windsor Castle. David Milford Haven arrived to enliven charades and other games, and Princess Margaret would subsequently inform Miss Crawford: 'David Milford Haven ... and Philip went mad.'

When staying in London Prince Philip now lived in an attic of the Mountbattens' latest home – 16 Chester Street, Belgravia. The house was strangely quiet, for Lord Louis was now in command of military operations in South-East Asia and Lady Mountbatten devoted much of her time to the Red Cross and St John Ambulance Services. It must have been with some relief, therefore, that in May 1944 Philip himself left for the Far East as the first lieutenant in the new destroyer *Whelp*. Forming part of the 27th Destroyer Flotilla under Admiral Sir James Somerville, the ship participated in the final operations against Japan. Thus Philip came under the supreme command of his uncle, Lord Mountbatten. Based mostly in Australia, Philip was a social success on a scale comparable only with that of his grandfather, Prince Louis of Battenberg. Such diversions punctuated the routine of long spells at sea. At the time of the catastrophe at Hiroshima, *Whelp* and her sister ship *Wager* were escorting Admiral Fraser's flagship, *Duke of York*, in company with the American fleet under Admiral Nimitz off Okinawa. The three British ships accompanied the *Missouri* for the historic surrender on 2 September 1945 in Tokyo Bay.

4

Confined to 'The Cage'

Returning to Portsmouth in January 1946, for the next three years Prince Philip's naval duties would keep him in England. During that period, from the virtual obscurity of a young naval officer he would be thrust under the fierce glare of world publicity. A slight ripple of public curiosity was stirred in May when he accompanied King George VI and Queen Elizabeth and their daughters at the wedding of the Hon. Mrs Vicary Gibbs to Captain the Hon. Andrew Elphinstone. In some minds there lingered the vague recollection that he was a protégé of the Mountbattens. But it is doubtful if many were impressed that he was a Greek prince, for members of the Greek Royal Family, who were then in London, were really no more than professional exiles. It was not generally appreciated that as a prince of the Royal House of Greece he was a great-nephew of Queen Alexandra and thus related in some way to Princess Elizabeth, the heir presumptive, with whom there appeared to be some familiarity. Indeed, unknown to the general public, Princess Elizabeth and Prince Philip had been seeing each other very much of late. Coppins, for instance, was a convenient rendezvous, for there the Princess could meet people in privacy on an equal basis.

There seems to be little doubt that Prince Philip was being carefully studied as a potential candidate for a delicate assignment: that of consort of a future queen. To some extent this was inevitable when it is realized that there was a marked paucity of acceptable suitors. To consider a German princeling during the immediate aftermath of war would have been hailed as an affront to the British people. As for Danish and Norwegian princes, they were not of an appropriate age. But what mattered the most – and was therefore the guiding factor – was public reaction. One had only to reflect on the fate of the last consort. Prince Albert, one of the most competent men of his time, had been unstinting in his services to Britain, a self-sacrificing dedication which had expedited his death. Yet the British people disliked him, more so because of his apparent lack of humanity. Therefore the next consort must, above all else, equal Prince Albert's talents but win widespread public approval. Moreover, he must embrace the Protestant faith.

Speculation of a possible romance was first stimulated in the newspapers by the gossip writers. Princess Elizabeth came increasingly under public scrutiny – at the theatre, dances and race meetings to which she was sometimes accompanied by young Guards officers. The public read that the Princess now possessed her own suite at Buckingham Palace overlooking the Mall – furnished in Victorian style, as a journalist revealed: 'It has soft easy chairs but the centre-piece is a business-like desk where the Princess writes her private letters and also attends to her growing official correspondence.' It was to this suite that Prince Philip sometimes came, driving his sports car into a back entrance at Buckingham Palace to avoid the inquisitive.

Prince Philip had been posted first as an instructor to the training establishment, HMS *Glendower*, at Pwllheli, and when this was closed down he and another officer organized HMS *Royal Arthur*, a similar station, at Corsham in Wiltshire. It was a cheerless place, a collection of temporary Nissen huts outside the little town. At the same time it was a challenge to Philip's progressive mind: he was inaugurating a programme which brought mariners' naval training in line with the requirements of the atomic age. When he now drove the ninety-eight miles from Corsham to London he was conscious that his movements were closely watched. Irritating though it was, for Prince Philip it was an early sampling of the constant strain confronting royalty. To evade the press, friends would sometimes invite Princess Elizabeth and Prince Philip to the privacy of their homes, and riding or walking in Windsor Great Park was another means of escape. Occasionally Philip would be the guest of ex-King Peter of Yugoslavia and Alexandra who occupied a house at Sunningdale with a private entrance into the Great Park.

Rumour fed on rumour. It was not merely the risk of hostile public reaction that the King had to cope with, but also the provocative Greek problem. Although Prince Philip had been reared in the British tradition, to many Britons – their xenophobia sharpened by war – he was still an alien. Rightly or wrongly, many people felt that Prince Philip could not be tolerated as a future consort. Doubtless there were some who thought that the future queen should marry a Briton. To them anyone from a British vintage family was preferable to the most eminent names in the *Almanach de Gotha*. Moreover, the King himself had married a commoner and severed the tradition by which British princes had contracted marriage with foreign brides.

When the *Sunday Pictorial* organized an opinion poll and forty per cent of readers voted against the choice of Philip as Princess Elizabeth's suitor, one had to take cognizance. However, reports suggest that King George of the Hellenes and Lord Mountbatten had no such qualms and exerted all the influence they could muster in Prince Philip's favour. Marriage to Alexandra was out of the question, for she was now the wife of Peter of Yugoslavia – a fact which is claimed to have been pointed out in a conversation in London between King George VI and King George of the Hellenes. In an indiscreet moment the Greek monarch referred in the hearing of others to a possible union between Elizabeth and Philip. It was a pity, he is alleged to have said, that Philip and Alexandra had not married, but it might be for the best, adding that it would be nice 'if we could reunite our families and countries through Lilibet and Philip'. To the annoyance of the British King, George of Greece is further credited with the words: 'It seems Lilibet is in love with Philip, and I know that he adores her.' Resenting the Greek sovereign's indiscretion in public, George VI replied in his halting manner: 'Philip had better not think any more about it at present. They are both too young.'

As Princess Elizabeth was only nineteen, the King and Queen thought that she was too young to be engaged. Queen Mary

Princess Alice of Battenberg, the mother of Prince Philip (and daughter of
Prince Louis of Battenberg, later the 1st Marquess of Milford Haven)
before her marriage to Prince Andrew of Greece.

Prince Alexander of Hesse-Darmstadt with his morganatic wife, Countess Julie von Hauke. She was eventually created Princess of Battenberg and thus founded the Battenberg (or Mountbatten) line.

Opposite
A childhood scene. Prince Philip (left) riding with his cousin, King Michael of Rumania, on the sands near Constanta.

King George I of the Hellenes and Queen Olga, founders of the Royal House of Greece, with Queen Alexandra (extreme right).

Dr Kurt Hahn, the German-born educationalist, who, as headmaster of Salem and Gordonstoun, was a major influence on the life of his royal pupil, Prince Philip.

Princess Elizabeth and Prince Philip, looking at their wedding photographs in the grounds of Broadlands, the Hampshire estate lent to them for their honeymoon by Lord and Lady Louis Mountbatten.

Two Italian boys conveying the Prince across a canal on the island of St Francisca, near Venice, during his final cruise in *Magpie* (known as 'Edinburgh's Private Yacht') before he left the Royal Navy.

A tiger shot by the Duke of Edinburgh during the royal tour of India. Critics cannot accept his apparent contradictions which permit him to kill wild life yet campaign to preserve it.

The Prince delights in exploring new places. He is shown chatting with a boy in the market in Rabat during an official visit to Morocco.

Part of Prince Philip's activities centre on recreational subjects for the young. The photograph illustrates a visit to the arts and crafts class at the Victoria Boys' and Girls' Clubs, Stamford Hill.

The Duke emerging from a Centurion tank in West Germany after he had fired about fifty shots. He was visiting the Queen's Royal Irish Hussars, of which he is commander-in-chief.

Some of the Prince's visits have a sombre aspect, as, for instance, when he went to the stricken village of Aberfan where 117 people had vanished beneath moving coal tips.

After presenting Council of Industrial Design Awards on board the *Queen Elizabeth 2*, Prince Philip inspected the liner's main control room.

Although the Prince accompanies the Queen at times of national ceremonial – as, for example, at the State Opening of Parliament – as Consort he holds no place in the constitution.

There are many facets to a Consort's life, such as the Trooping the Colour ceremony to celebrate the Queen's official birthday. The Duke is talking with Mrs D A Houblon, stand-in for the Queen during a rehearsal.

Prince Philip's passion for sports ranks down the centuries with other royal enthusiasts. He has now abandoned the polo field for less arduous pursuits.

Piloting a helicopter of the Queen's Flight himself, Philip, accompanied by Prince Andrew and Prince Edward, inspected the latest in helicopter design at Dunsborough Park, Ripley.

The Queen and Prince Philip relaxing on the Balmoral estate.

A royal barbecue at Balmoral. Prince Philip prepares a meal with the aid of Princess Anne.

The First Gentleman of the Realm with the heir apparent. Prince Philip has been a powerful influence in the training of Prince Charles for his future duties as monarch.

Relaxing during a bird-photographing expedition to Hilbre Island on the Cheshire Dee.

confided in Lady Airlie: 'They want her to see more of the world before committing herself, and to see more men.' Lady Airlie pointed out that she herself had fallen in love when nineteen and it had been permanent. 'Yes, it does sometimes happen,' replied the old Queen, 'and Elizabeth seems to be that kind of girl. She would always know her own mind. There is something very steadfast and determined in her – like her father.'

It was not that the King objected to Philip; indeed, in his view the Prince had a dynamic personality, and once remarked: 'I like Philip. He is intelligent, he has a good sense of humour and thinks about things the right way.' He reasoned, however, that his daughter had met too few eligible young men and should not be committed.

Whether or not he became the consort of a future queen, Prince Philip wished to pursue his naval career. But no permanent commissions were granted to aliens in peacetime. Yet when he had tried to become a British citizen filling in form s– 'for aliens in the Fighting Services' – nothing had transpired. At the end of 1944, the King of the Hellenes had given his blessing to naturalization, and all that now remained, it seemed, were the formal discussions with a pliant Home Office. But the irritations of diplomatic communications intervened. Greece had been rent by civil war. Churchill and Eden had visited Athens on Christmas Day 1944, extracting from the turmoil a fragile peace and the appointment of Archbishop Damaskinos as Regent. But was the King of the Hellenes ever to be allowed to return to his throne? In London, official reaction was hesitant; to grant naturalization to a member of the Greek Royal Family might incur a fierce political backlash if it seemed that Britain wholeheartedly shored up the royal cause. On the other hand, it might also be thought that the future of the Royal Family seemed so gloomily precarious as to need sanctuary in Britain. In the summer of 1946 the fate of the Greek Royal Family hung in the balance. From bitter wrangling and recriminations resulted a plebiscite as to the King's return. Although sixty per cent of his subjects had voted in his favour, there was the sobering inexorable truth that forty per cent had voted against or expressed indifference. Ominously the Communists, backed by the Soviet Union, were tightening a ruthless grip. For the Greek monarchy the signs appeared to convey foreboding.

In the circumstances, it was believed in London that it might be an embarrassment to allow naturalization so soon after the restoration – an attitude which, if one writer is correct, met with the disfavour of Lord Mountbatten, who reminded George VI of Queen Victoria's interests in the Battenbergs. (He might have added that Philip's Danish ancestry, the Schleswig–Holstein–Sondersburg–Glücksburg line, had already provided three consorts for British sovereigns – wives for James I and Edward VII and a husband for Queen Anne – a fine record by any standards.) However, it was not solely a matter for George VI; it concerned the politicians too. In confidential talks the King secured the views of Prime Minister Clement Attlee, Winston Churchill (then leader of the Opposition), who was in favour of a betrothal, Lord Jowitt (the Lord Chancellor) and Chuter Ede (the Home Secretary) as to the political and constitutional implications if Princess Elizabeth became engaged to a Greek prince.

Outwardly the prospects looked dark for Philip. In Greece a tottering throne was propped up precariously by British troops, whose support for an allegedly cruel administration created international friction. In Britain, the Socialist Party – even the Attlee Cabinet – was in conflict. Conveying in a published statement their profound sense of horror over events in Greece, eighty-six Labour Left-wing back-benchers condemned the Greek royal regime for 'barbaric atrocities'. With the political temperature so high in Socialist quarters the engagement of Princess Elizabeth to Prince Philip was held to be inopportune.

The romance, however, was by no means on the wane. On 19 August 1946, Prince Philip's name appeared in the King's Game Book at Balmoral and in the Court Circular; with four more guests, George VI had invited him to participate in grouse shooting over Tomboddies and Blairglas. But for Philip the occasion would be more momentous in its impact on his life. Queen Mary once confided to Lady Airlie: 'I believe Elizabeth fell in love with Philip the first time he went down to Windsor.' That may be so, but it was at Balmoral in that mellow mid-August that Elizabeth heard Philip's proposal and accepted. In her diary, her great-great-grandmother Queen Victoria describes how she had thanked her future consort for 'his self-sacrifice'. No record exists of what Princess Elizabeth remarked at her betrothal, but some years later she disclosed that the proposal occurred 'beside some well-loved loch, the white clouds sailing overhead and the curlew crying'.

The King and Queen accepted Prince Philip as their future son-in-law, but George VI firmly insisted on the postponement of a formal announcement for some while – certainly until after the forthcoming royal visit to South Africa. Princess Elizabeth and Princess Margaret were to accompany their parents and perhaps it was reckoned that absence from Philip would test her affection. Some of the King's advisers, it is said, were still against the match.

In view of the secrecy, it was the more embarrassing to Palace officials when the royal Greek newspaper *Hellenicon Aema* published in September an account of the 'impending announcement of the betrothal of Princess Elizabeth to Prince Philip of Greece'. There is an irrepressible belief that the disclosure was deliberately engineered and that King George of the Hellenes, willingly or coerced by his government, was endeavouring to use the British Royal Family as an instrument to ward off approaching disaster. Whether the innuendo is uncharitable or not, there was consternation at Buckingham Palace and 10 Downing Street. In Britain, in response to a clamouring press, it was ambiguously denied that any 'engagement of Her Royal Highness has been announced'. Seen in perspective over the years the denial might seem absurd today, for in the following month Elizabeth and Philip were photographed together for the first time – somewhat ironically at the wedding of Earl Mountbatten's daughter to Lord Brabourne at Romsey Abbey. The press appeared to be blessed with proper insight. With the couple stood the King, but when the photograph was published throughout the world, His Majesty had been deleted. The curiosity of the British public was now complete, and when

Prince Philip spent Christmas with the Royal Family at Sandringham many interpreted its true significance.

When the Royal Family left in the battleship *Vanguard* on
1 February 1947, life grew somewhat tedious for Prince Philip.
The absence of the Royal Family coincided with a period of
strong blizzards which swept post-war Britain, blocking roads
and railway tracks and bringing many factories to a halt. Elec-
trical power was switched off for long periods, taxing the resilience and patience of the people. Very soon the elements
wrought havoc with the country's precarious economy. It was
not the ideal atmosphere in which to foster public acceptance of
a royal engagement. For Philip, now that Uncle Dickie and
Aunt Edwina had left for India, the house in Chester Street
was virtually silent. In some slight way Prince Philip became
identified with Lord Mountbatten's mission to India. For years
the varied peoples on the Indian sub-continent had demanded
autonomy, and in December 1946 Attlee requested Mountbatten to become the twenty-ninth (and, as events proved, the
last) Viceroy of India. The primary object was to unravel the
sub-continent's tangled political and social skein, but to Tory
and other opponents of self-government Mountbatten was condemned as 'the grave-digger of the Indian empire'.

Mountbatten rejected Attlee's offer when he was first
approached and conflicting opinions have been suggested as to
the reason. It has been claimed that as a high-ranking naval
officer, he preferred to devote his obvious skills to the career to
which he had dedicated himself. But there is also a less benevolent interpretation, claiming that Lord Mountbatten's over-
riding passion was to break down any obstruction to Philip's
engagement to the heiress to the throne. For instance, in his
biography of King George VI, John W. Wheeler Bennett
claimed emphatically that 'as far back as 1944, four years
before Elizabeth's marriage, Lord Mountbatten was urging his
nephew's desire'.

A more feasible explanation was forthcoming from Earl
Mountbatten himself when, addressing Rotarians in London
in November 1951, he remarked: 'When Mr Attlee asked me

to go to India as Viceroy, I at first told him that my answer was no. I said that nobody in his right frame of mind would dream of going out to try and solve an insoluble problem. I then found that His Majesty himself was sold on the idea, and it was the King who next asked me to take on the job. I am sure you will agree that once the King asks you to do a job, nobody can say no. So I took it.'

It is difficult to accept that the King's actions were politically motivated. Ever since the abdication of his brother Edward VIII, he had been acutely sensitive to the privileges and obligations of monarchy. King Edward's romance with Mrs Simpson had divided the nation for a while and almost wrecked the throne. Once again, the people of Britain were just as vehemently split over the Greek affair and in his wisdom he had no wish to expose his daughter to controversy. A formula had therefore to be devised to avoid it.

This materialized while the King was still in South Africa. Clement Attlee and Lord Jowitt appreciated that if Philip was to wed the heiress to the British throne, he must win the people's plaudits as a British subject, and not as a prince of Greece; naturalization and total renunciation of his hereditary claim to the Greek throne (which in any event was tenuous) and any other dynastic rights. Such action would sever Philip from the Greek royal house and the much maligned administration in Athens. In the circumstances, he would be aloof from the type of abuse which had resulted many years earlier in King Constantine's downfall. Furthermore, as he anticipated, Attlee was in consequence able to appease the critics in the Socialist Party. In that way, the politicians won over public acceptance generally. But naturalization not only deprived Philip of his princely titles; he also had no surname, for both the royal families of Denmark and Greece use no family name. It was considered out of the question, however, that the heiress presumptive should marry a commoner. At the College of Heralds it was suggested that Philip should receive the title of 'Prince of Oldcastle' – an anglicized version of Oldenburg, the name of the German dukes from whom emanated the Danish Royal Family. But this, it seems, did not sound quite right, and, one writer contends, was certainly not harmonious to the ears of Earl Mountbatten.

Although it is customary for people to take the surname of their father – an argument which would be submitted in Philip's favour when, in due course, the name of his own descendants was debated – King George VI was recommended to approve the maiden name of Princess Alice, his mother. This idea has been attributed to Mr Chuter Ede, the one-time school teacher and then the Socialist Home Secretary. Advocating the name of Mountbatten, he remarked: 'It is certainly grander and more glittering than Oldcastle.' A British title was also mooted, but on his own choice Philip rejected the proposal; he desired, he explained, to be known simply as Lieutenant Philip Mountbatten, R.N. But this could be only temporary; by the time he stood at the altar with his bride, he would be a duke.

Prince Philip's naturalization occurred on 18 March 1947, roughly a month before Princess Elizabeth attained her twenty-first birthday. The Royal Family was still in South Africa. His name appeared in a heterogeneous list of 880 – of Poles and other aliens, including German Jewish refugees – that appeared in the *London Gazette*, and his registration fee of £10 was defrayed by the Home Office. As a naval officer he was not compelled to swear an oath of allegiance, for since Stuart times a member of the Royal Navy is automatically accepted as the sovereign's servant. This is not so in the Army – once the instrument of Parliament – where it is imperative to declare loyalty. Curiously the announcement of Prince Philip's naturalization roused scant interest, but within four months as a personality he would be known world wide. Today it can be seen that fate was extremely perverse. It is now accepted that Prince Philip need not have applied for naturalization. Indeed, he was a British subject from the outset. This was substantiated by the legal case, 'Attorney-General *v.* Prince Ernest Augustus of Hanover', whereby all descendants of the Electress of Hanover are British subjects by virtue of the Act of 1705 passed in the reign of Queen Anne.

The pressure increased for Philip between now and the wedding at Westminster Abbey on 20 November. The ubiquitous press tenaciously – and not without much irritation to himself – dogged his movements, and when his car skidded and struck a tree one wet night he was publicly rebuked for endangering his fiancée's happiness. Philip, who was returning from London to Corsham, twisted a knee. A passing motorist – a woman driver – took him to Cirencester. Censured one newspaper: 'Lieutenant Mountbatten's well-being is essential to the happiness of the heir to the Throne. Lieutenant Mountbatten should take care.' The incident occurred only four weeks from the wedding.

Soon Philip bore the stigma of being a reckless driver and especially when, after their marriage, his car – in which the Princess was a passenger – hit the wing of a London taxi. For a while, an outcry would try to ban him from driving the heiress to the throne. True or not, it was insinuated that the Palace chauffeurs resented occupying a car with Philip; he was addicted to speed. If that is true he shared a foible with Edward VII who used to admonish his chauffeur: 'Faster, Stamper. Faster!'

By now Prince Philip had dispensed with the clandestine practice of sending letters to Princess Elizabeth through the medium of a lady-in-waiting. He now openly corresponded care of Buckingham Palace. And when an official in the Palace Post Office leaked to the press the news of the regular flow of mail to and from South Africa, the pretence that no engagement was pending had grown into a farce. The time to end all make-believe was overdue. After the Royal Family returned from South Africa in May, Elizabeth and Philip were seen frequently together in West End restaurants and night clubs, and on 10 July 1947, after Commonwealth governments had been acquainted, King George VI announced his consent to the marriage.

On the day of the official engagement Sir Harold Nicolson, King George V's biographer, attended a Buckingham Palace garden party and revealed: 'Everybody is straining to see the bridal pair – irreverently and shamelessly straining.'

To help Philip cope with his mounting mail, the Mountbattens' secretary, Miss Lees, visited him at the Marchioness of Milford Haven's apartment at Kensington Palace, where he now stayed when in London. John Dean, the young butler at Chester Street, who served him and David Milford Haven as valet, has explained that their rooms were 'astonishingly poor and humble – not at all what one would expect in a palace. The floors were scrubbed boards, with rather worn rugs'.

Philip's rise to international prominence had been fantastic and although his expenses had not soared proportionately, at least they were now outside the scope of a naval lieutenant's pay. There has been the strong hint that, for the moment, the Mountbattens eased the financial strain. To what extent Philip benefited from his late father's estate (if at all), it is hard to assess. In 1946 he journeyed to Monte Carlo to finalize Prince Andrew's affairs. It has been reported that after his father's debts and funeral expenses had been disbursed little remained in the estate. Prince Philip returned to London with a few mementoes, among them items of clothing and an ivory-handled shaving brush. There were also the technical formalities of a probate case to conclude. From King George I, his father, Prince Andrew had been entitled to estates in Greece. Formal litigation arranged on behalf of Prince Andrew of Greece, deceased, by the executors, the London solicitors, Rehder and Higgs, against Philip of Greece in the Chancery Division, awarded Philip, it is said, with extremely modest funds.

Philip's personal assets were far from excessive. According to John Dean, on Philip's arrival at Kensington Palace, 'the young Naval officer brought all his worldly belongings in two suit-cases'. To his valet's surprise, the Prince did not even possess a pair of proper hair brushes. According to one writer, Prince Philip must have been one of the poorest citizens in Britain at the time of his engagement. He explained: 'One of the more senior officials at Buckingham Palace who wrote his memoirs after he retired [though they have not so far been published] mentioned in one of the chapters that Prince Philip was "as poor as a church mouse" when he first proposed to Princess Elizabeth. All he possessed was his uniform, a spare suit and a credit of £6 10s 0d at the bank.'

This assessment of Prince Philip's material wealth utterly ignores the fundamental qualities that he possessed, which cannot be gauged in financial terms. He was a young man of un-restrained vitality (which would be misrepresented by carping critics at times as exhibitionism or bumptiousness) and a lively – even magnetic personality – which could not be ignored. He had reached an age when one could note the crystallization of all the influences which had so far moulded his personality. The qualities were inborn but had proved malleable under the skill of others. The maternal characteristics were patent: a resilience and determination to face challenge and endure hardship. The ability to charm and communicate with ease were probably in-herited from his father. Perhaps there has been too much em-phasis on the loneliness of childhood to account for the zeal and tenacity to learn and succeed in whatever he essays. Pro-bably it is nearer the truth to say that the drive and dynamism were assets consolidated under the rigours of Gordonstoun and naval training. Lesser capabilities have enabled men to amass fortunes and rise to distinction in many spheres of life. There is nothing to imply that Prince Philip himself has ever under-valued his own mental capacities or that he ever considered them to be inept for the role of consort. In this he has been proved to be right not only throughout the twenty-five years of the Queen's reign but throughout their marriage.

Ironically for Philip, although he had entered this world as a Prince, fate had so far deprived him of the financial means to live like one. But now marriage would change that. Obviously a naval lieutenant's pay of about £11 weekly, plus a wife's allowance of £4 7s 6d, would not suffice. King George VI approached Parliament – 'relying on the liberality and affection of my faithful Commons' – and Herbert Morrison, then Leader of the House, chose a Select Committee to suggest provision. Clearly there was no unanimity in discussions; by thirteen votes to five it was agreed to allocate an annuity of £10,000 to Philip, with an increased annuity of £50,000 for Princess Eliza-beth, both allowances to be subject to income tax. (Since then these figures have been greatly increased.) Doubtless Philip was the victim of Sir Stafford Cripps's austerity measures, for Prince Albert, the consort of Queen Victoria, had received treble that sum in an age when the purchasing power of the pound was tenfold. The King reacted by surrendering £100,000 tax free saved in wartime economies on the Civil List.

Also of some urgency to Prince Philip was the question of an engagement ring. Considering that the Royal Family own perhaps the world's most fabulous private collection of jewels, how could he offer something in keeping? He had been saving from his naval pay to the point that brother officers unwittingly thought him niggardly. But the amount that had accrued was not enough. His mother, Princess Alice, rallied to his aid. Most of her personal jewels had disappeared in the cause of philanthropy, yet she had retained her engagement ring – the gift of Prince Andrew – and a diamond ring which had been owned by her grandmother. Princess Alice was living temporarily with her mother at Kensington Palace, the Greek Communists having finally ejected the Greek Royal Family, but not before Princess Alice had stubbornly declined British protection until her orphans in Athens had been adequately safeguarded. She herself sketched designs for the proposed ring and showed them to Philip, then one day visited the fourth-floor showroom of a Bond Street jewellers. Although for practical reasons her design was eventually modified, finally there emerged a solitaire diamond with diamond shoulders set in platinum. Prince Philip did not need to buy a wedding ring either. For that purpose the people of Wales supplied a nugget of gold.

The King gave the young couple a grace-and-favour home – Sunninghill Park near Ascot. The mansion bore scars from its wartime use by the Army and an enemy bomb. Yet it could boast of grandiose features, especially the exquisite marble staircase, and not far away stretched a tree-fringed lake. Unfortunately, however, before restoration could begin, the house was mysteriously gutted by fire. Arson was suspected, but this the police would neither contradict nor confirm.

The King now allowed Princess Elizabeth and Prince Philip the future use of Clarence House, a huge square mansion facing the Mall and St James's Park. On this occasion Parliament was much more generous, voting £50,000 for its restoration. Once the residence of the Duke of Clarence (who became William IV), it had been derelict and unoccupied for thirty years, apart from serving as a war-time home for the British Red Cross. Clarence House, where another Duchess of Edinburgh – the Russian princess who married Victoria's second son – had also resided, was antiquated even by Victorian standards. But gradually out of the dust and rubble would emerge an exquisite home, with a neighbouring house in Ambassadors' Court serving as domestic and secretarial offices. Whilst the renovations were in progress, Elizabeth and Philip would live after their marriage in the Princess's apartment at Buckingham Palace before taking over the Earl of Athlone's quarters at Kensington Palace, when he left to be Governor-General of South Africa. For week-ends they would rent Windlesham Moor in Surrey, near Windsor.

All this time the pressures for Princess Elizabeth and Prince Philip intensified. There was also the question of Philip's religion. Dr Geoffrey Fisher, Archbishop of Canterbury, wrote to the King:

'There is a matter upon which I should consult Your Majesty. There was a paragraph in *The Times* which said that while Lieutenant Mountbatten was baptised into the Greek Orthodox Church he appears "always to have regarded himself as an Anglican". The same paragraph also misrepresented the relations between the Church of England and the Orthodox Church ...

'In the Church of England we are always ready to minister to members of the Orthodox Church and to admit to the Sacrament. No difficulty therefore arises of any sort on our side from the fact that Lieutenant Mountbatten was baptised into the Orthodox Church. At the same time, unless he is officially received into the Church of England he remains formally a member of the Greek Orthodox Church, which, though on the closest and most friendly terms with us, is not able to enter into full communion with us. If it be true that Lieutenant Mountbatten has always regarded himself as an Anglican I suggest for Your Majesty's consideration that there would be an advantage if he were officially received into the Church of England. It can be done privately and very simply ... I will most willingly discuss it further with

you, or, if Your Majesty thinks fit, with Lieutenant Mountbatten.'

Philip was received into the Anglican Church at a private
ceremony.

In striking contrast to the simple demands of the Anglican
Church were the protests and controversy over the wedding
plans. Post-war austerity was at its peak. Queues and rationing
symbolized the nature of daily life. Not unnaturally the Royal
Family and the Labour Government thought that only an
austere wedding would be acceptable to the nation. Initially
it was proposed to solemnize the wedding at St George's
Chapel, Windsor (where King Edward VII had been married)
or in the Chapel Royal at St James's Palace (where Queen
Victoria had married Prince Albert). But the suggestion was
loudly scoffed at by many, headed by the Tory politicians in
both the House of Lords and the House of Commons. The
people, it was argued, were satiated by the humdrum mono-
tony of life and yearned for colour and romance. 'The glamour
of it all,' an American journalist rightly summed up, 'in the
midst of Britain's drab existence nowadays, has jerked millions
out of their one-candlepower lives and tossed them into dream-
land.' The forthcoming wedding also had a dynamic effect on
people abroad. The *New York Herald-Tribune* described 'the
way, which no egalitarian American can understand, the British
Crown binds together the British people', and the *New York
Times* enthused over 'this welcome occasion for gaiety in grim
England, beset in peace with troubles almost as burdensome as
those of the war'.

There were a few strident notes to jar the national rejoicing.
Perhaps most piercing of all was the resolution sent to King
George by the Camden Town First Branch of the Amalgamated
Society of Woodworkers. It read:

'It is wished to remind you that any banqueting and display
of wealth at your daughter's wedding will be an insult to the
British people at the present time, and we consider that you
would be well advised to order a very quiet wedding in

keeping with the times.... May we also remind you that
should you declare the wedding day a public holiday you will
have a word beforehand with the London Master Builders'
Association to ensure that we are paid for it.'

In all the national emotion, the trivia and spate of correspondence in the newspapers, news relating specifically to
Philip was conspicuously absent. Even John Masefield, the
Poet Laureate, completely ignored the groom in his wedding-
day ode, which ended:

> To such a Crown all broken spirits turn:
> And we, who see this young face passing by,
> See her as Symbol of a Power Etern,
> And pray that Heaven may bless her till she die.

To Philip it must have seemed that he was an observer rather
than one of the two principals concerned. It was not until the
eve of the wedding that he really appeared on the nuptial scene,
when he was restored to the ranks of the titled. Probably he
favoured the fact that the name of Mountbatten would from
now onwards receive less prominence, for he is on record as
saying: '... one impression that I think needs to be corrected
is that ... I was brought up by Lord Mountbatten ... and that
I am a Mountbatten, which of course I am not. I mean, I am
a Mountbatten in exactly the same way that everybody else
is half mother and half father, but normally speaking you are
concerned with the father's family. I don't think anybody
thinks I had a father. Most people think that Dickie's my father
anyway.' One account asserts that Philip himself was not
'greatly in favour' of being given Mountbatten as his surname.
It smacked too much of the celebrated uncle, and Philip, complete in himself, has quite rightly preferred to be his own mouse
rather than another person's lion. ('But in the end I was persuaded, and anyway I could not think of a reasonable alterna-
tive.') Even when the Queen changed her married surname of
Mountbatten back to Windsor, Philip, it appears, considered
that the change of patrimony would have been more appro-

priate in the title 'Family of Windsor of the House of Edinburgh'.

Until his naturalization, Prince Philip had never possessed a surname. Like his parents when they discussed names for his christening, for him plain 'Philip' was enough. But it would sometimes be a disability, as on the occasion he hired a car in Australia while on shore-leave. The disbelieving garage-hand would not accept simply the name 'Philip' and there was suspicion and mounting annoyance when he added 'Prince of Greece'. Similarly he had shrunk from pandering to the collectors of autographs. This dates back to the Gordonstoun days when an autograph hunter requested his signature and was astonished to read 'Baldwin of Bewdley'. There was also the embarrassing incident during Prince Philip's visit to an RAF station in Western Germany. Affability had been the key-note throughout the proceedings until the farewell, when the commanding officer held out a copy of the day's programme for signature. 'This is not usual,' Prince Philip said icily. On this occasion he signed, then without further ado boarded his aircraft. The warden at St George's House, Windsor, was less fortunate. As the menu cards signed by the various guests began to mount on reaching Prince Philip, the Warden requested him to add his signature and pass them on. 'I am not a pop star,' Philip remarked quietly.

On 19 November 1947, on the eve of his wedding, George VI granted Philip rank and status suitable for the husband of the heiress presumptive. At a private investiture at Buckingham Palace, King George installed him a Knight Commander of the Most Noble Order of the Garter. (Whether or not he wished to guarantee seniority – an insinuation that has been made – the King had invested Princess Elizabeth eight days earlier.) Sir Philip Mountbatten was then created Duke of Edinburgh, Earl of Merioneth and Baron Greenwich. Happily the Dukedom was the revival of a title that disappeared on the death in 1900 of Queen Victoria's son Alfred, Duke of Edinburgh, who had facilitated the entry of Philip's grandfather, Prince Louis of Battenberg, into the Royal Navy.

Philip was also entitled to the honorifico of 'His Royal High-

ness', yet quite strangely King George VI did not create him a
British prince. It has since been implied that this was an over-
sight, but it has also been claimed that it was 'done on the
advice of Mr Attlee and others who feared the popular effect of
too much too soon'. (Not until ten years elapsed – on 22 February 1957 – would the Queen declare that the Duke 'shall henceforth be known as His Royal Highness The Prince Philip, Duke
of Edinburgh'.)

A fortnight before the wedding King George had written to
his mother, Queen Mary, about the titles Philip was to receive,
observing: 'It is a great deal to give a man all at once, but I
know Philip understands his new responsibilities on his
marriage to Lilibet.' Cynics have mischievously hinted that the
title of prince was deliberately withheld to deflate Philip of his
conceit. Again, the argument is invalid considering that at the
outset, despite the King's offer of titles, it was Philip himself
who abandoned them to become plain Lieutenant Philip
Mountbatten. King Frederick X of Denmark appointed him an
honorary lieutenant in the Danish Navy and conferred the
Order of the Elephant on both Elizabeth and Philip.

The numerous wedding gifts that also reached the Prince
and Princess from all over the world were exhibited in St
James's Palace to raise funds for charity. During a visit to the
display Prince Philip gave a foretaste of his uninhibited candour. Among the presents was a gift from Mahatma Gandhi
which Queen Mary misunderstood as being a loincloth.
Amazed, she remarked: 'What a horrible thing!' 'I don't think
it's horrible,' exclaimed Philip. 'Gandhi is a wonderful man, a
very great man.' Actually at Lord Mountbatten's request,
Gandhi, whirring his spinning-wheel, had spun a table-mat to
his own design.

On the night before the wedding Commander Norfolk, who
had been captain of *Whelp*, supervised Philip's bachelor dinner
at the Dorchester Hotel. Present were Philip's best man, his
cousin David, Lieutenant-Commander Parker, Baron, the
Court photographer, who had introduced Philip to a favourite
haunt, the Thursday Club, other young naval officers and Earl
Mountbatten, to whom is attributed the arrival of the press.

In their next issues the London daily newspapers regaled readers with their accounts of hilarious scenes, and numerous people lying on the cold pavements – waiting patiently to witness the wedding procession that day – were totally ignorant that a car which passed them in the early hours of the morning contained the bridegroom. Despite the carousal, when Philip was roused by his valet at seven, he was found to be in 'great form [and] extremely cheerful'. It was a cold dismal day and Philip invited the press to take coffee with him before he left for the Palace. Wearing his naval uniform, by his side hung the sword of his grandfather Prince Louis. But contrary to a widespread misconception, Prince Louis had not worn it at his wedding. Dressed in the uniform of the Royal Hessian Artillery, he had carried a sabre.

The ceremony, at which the bride wore a gown studded with ten thousand pearls, coruscated the drab, blitzed London scene. But one rather sad omission marred the proceedings for Prince Philip. Whilst Princess Alice, temporarily discarding her nun-like costume in favour of a lace gown and plumed toque, witnessed both the marriage and the subsequent signing of the register, regrettably, Prince Philip's sisters were absent. The presence of German princesses so soon after the war, advisers warned King George, might inflame the public. The rumour that one sister actually attended incognito is groundless. The truth is that all three met at Marienburg Castle, south of Hanover, the ancestral home of Sophie's second husband, Prince George of Hanover. Later they learnt that Philip had signed the wedding register with their joint gift, a gold fountain-pen engraved with their names, which he uses on formal occasions. No one can say with accuracy what the public's reaction would have been, but Prince George had the right to be present even though he was a German prince. As the brother of Prince Ernest Augustus, he was actually entitled to British nationality. This complex situation amused Princess Alice who once exclaimed that since Prince George's sister was her niece, Queen Frederika, then the former Queen of Greece, might be legally a British national.

The Mountbattens lent Broadlands, their Hampshire estate,

to the young couple for their honeymoon. A two-coach special train took the newly-weds with Princess Elizabeth's maid, Miss Bobo MacDonald, and Prince Philip's valet, John Dean, to Winchester, where they were welcomed by ecstatic crowds. The choice of Broadlands, however, was disastrous; the only peace they would experience would be in their suite – decorated in a tasteful blend of white and pale grey, with delicate eighteenth-century furniture and Dali sketches. Here, incidentally, in these same rooms, the Mountbattens had also begun their honeymoon.

Public reaction was so overwhelming that it destroyed all chances of privacy. Even the combined efforts of the local police and London security men were too meagre to tackle the ubiquitous sightseers and photographers, who even hid in the trees. British royalty will tolerate much, but peeping Toms are sternly rebuffed. For instance, at the Prince of Wales's wedding Disraeli, directing his quizzing-glass at Queen Victoria, wilted before the sovereign's withering gaze. Absurd intrusion likewise enraged Philip. When out shooting pheasants, he was sorely tempted to direct his fire at two intruders lurking in a tree. To Philip the honeymoon indicated that even if there was no place in the constitution for a consort, one of his tasks would be to protect his wife from unnecessary strain. This he would accomplish during the Queen's reign.

When the intolerable point was reached whereby privacy became impossible, Princess Elizabeth and Prince Philip escaped to the seclusion of Scotland. Calling first at Buckingham Palace, Philip issued a statement which, intended or not, seemed ambiguous: 'The reception given us on our wedding day and the loving interest shown by our fellow countrymen ... have left an impression that will never grow faint. We can find no words to express what we feel, but we can at least offer our grateful thanks to the millions who have given us this unforgettable send-off in our married life.' Although the weather had deteriorated, Elizabeth and Philip found peace on Deeside – at Birkhall, a Georgian house not far from Balmoral which was originally purchased for Edward VII.

While still on her honeymoon, Princess Elizabeth received a

letter from the King, who wrote: 'Our family, us four, the "Royal Family" must remain together with additions of course at suitable moments! I have watched you grow up in these years with pride under the skilful direction of Mummy, who as you know is the most marvellous person in the world in my eyes, & I can I know, always count on you, & now Philip, to help us in our work.' He was relieved that his daughter had admitted that the long wait before the engagement had been appropriate, and added: 'I can see that you are sublimely happy with Philip which is right but do not forget us.'

Princess Elizabeth and Prince Philip returned south for King George's birthday on 14 December, and spent a family Christmas at Sandringham. This was Philip's second visit to the Norfolk estate, and now that he was a fully-fledged member of the family, he was obliged to adhere to the tradition of wearing a kilt. The King showed him several which had been worn by King George v, and Philip selected one of the most colourful – Stuart hunting tartan. But even after adjustment the tartan was much too short. Philip felt ridiculous and, it is said, in a facetious moment curtsied to his father-in-law, a pleasantry which evoked a spontaneous rebuke from the King who, though not lacking in humour, was a stickler for etiquette.

Public duties followed immediately in the wake of the honeymoon, but unlike Prince Albert, who became consort the moment he married Queen Victoria, Prince Philip would enjoy four years of semi-freedom before he was totally confined to what Queen Wilhelmina of the Netherlands once called 'The Cage'. It was a period which, to quote Prince Albert, enabled Prince Philip to establish himself as 'the master in the house'. Albert was deploring (though he would have no foundation for complaint in due course) his status as the husband but not the master in Victoria's homes. At this juncture Philip would not be so humiliated. 'Within the house, and whatever we did, it was together,' he has since revealed. 'I suppose I naturally filled the principal position.' To his later annoyance, his thorny problems would begin only on Princess Elizabeth's accession. Meanwhile, as Lieutenant-Commander Parker, his private secretary at that time, explained, Prince Philip served 'as a kind of super chief of staff' who enlightened Princess Elizabeth when possible, giving her 'the complete lowdown on absolutely anything'. With or without the companionship of Princess Elizabeth, Philip was contributing his quota to the multifarious functions to which royalty are invited. While he was not averse to collaborating in these exacting yet often boring tasks, he stressed that his true desire was to pursue his career in the navy. He had been assured of a sinecure naval appointment because of his new status but he rejected it, arguing trenchantly that he could accept promotion solely on merit. The King was sympathetic.

Soon after his marriage Prince Philip had been appointed to the Operations Division of the Admiralty as its youngest member, a distinction that persisted when to Philip's joy he was instructed in April 1948 to take a naval course at Greenwich. This was tangible proof that the Admiralty viewed him as potential material for high rank. Yet when all the signs augured well for Prince Philip's naval future, a serious vascular obstruction was discovered that affected the King's legs. At one point there was the grave fear that the right leg would have to be removed. Fortunately this was avoided, but finally seven doctors had to operate on the King to by-pass the affected artery. During George VI's inactivity many more duties devolved on the Duke of Gloucester and Prince Philip. But it seems there was need to 'embellish his [Philip's] image'. According to one writer the task of the Palace advisers was to 'build him up into a public figure because for a time he was unsure of himself'. This is given as the reason for his appointment as president of the National Playing Fields Association in 1949. It is purported that Earl Mountbatten had retained at the Admiralty and as Viceroy in India staff who had served him during the war. Among them were public relations experts who suggested that Earl Mountbatten should resign from one of his part-time appointments in favour of his nephew. In that way Prince Philip would be offered the breakthrough 'in his campaign to win the solid approval of the British people'.

One finds it difficult to believe that with such an assertive personality Philip required an injection of confidence. At his initial meeting as president, he informed the committee: 'Gentlemen, I want to assure you that I have no intention of being a sitting tenant in this post.' Owing to the intervention of the war, the organization had begun to creak and needed to be oiled. There was also the red tape to disentangle and, above all, the need to convince the public that it deserved their support. That was the flagrant demand: financially the movement was anaemic and in need of a cash transfusion.

Prince Philip's passion for sport and the ideals implanted in him at Gordonstoun attracted him all the more to the Association's objectives. He urged everyone to strive for stability, working many hours himself, issuing appeals, and 'squeezing all the rich people I know for all the juice I can get out of them'. He extracted support from industry, the public and the worlds of sport and show business, either in the form of cheques or service. Frank Sinatra flew to London for a show at the Albert Hall that raised £16,000. And when Prince Philip co-starred with Bob Hope, the comedian, in a film depicting poor London children whose playgrounds were the streets, that alone raised £84,000. Altogether in four years the coffers teemed with more than £500,000. Philip was not prepared to be just a name on the letter-heads. Completing the staff course at Greenwich, for a while he attended the Association's offices in Buckingham Gate daily. He assured that he would 'go anywhere to open a new playing field', and put his words into practice, travelling many thousands of miles annually.

Having planned the money-raising schemes, he not unreasonably decided on the allocations. He toured Britain making speeches, coercing the faint-hearted and the hesitant, prodding them to buy derelict land for recreational purposes, and spoke forthrightly to municipal planners. For instance: 'You may believe that you have designed the perfect playing field as seen through adult eyes, but I can assure you that it may prove deadly dull to a child of four.' His presidency would continue until 1972, his longest term of office. Normally he does not believe in lengthy official associations for fear that staleness sets in, but he was anxious to bring pleasure to children deprived of the normal opportunities for recreational happiness. In the process, Prince Philip became the first member of the Royal Family since King Edward VII to be intimately connected with show business. He has enjoyed it and it has been a profitable source to tap. In November 1949, exactly one month after the fund-raising Variety Club was founded, he was appointed a Life Clown. Even when Philip resumed his naval career at Malta – due to an improvement in the King's health – he corresponded with the NPFA.

He arrived in the Mediterranean on 17 October 1949 for duty as first lieutenant of the flotilla leader *Chequers*. Lord Mountbatten, who was then commanding the first cruiser squadron, welcomed Philip at the airport – 'as an uncle not as an admiral', he prudently told the press. When possible Princess Elizabeth joined her husband. Their hosts were the Mountbattens at the Villa Guardamangia, with its vine-hung terraces, lemon trees and red earth. When eventually Lord Louis returned to London as Fourth Sea Lord, the villa was leased in the Princess's name and the Clarence House staff shipped out plate and linen. The period spent in Malta – by royal standards simple and carefree – was perhaps the happiest phase of their married lives; never again would they live casually like ordinary people. When in port Prince Philip spent much time at home, rising at 6.30 a.m. to be on board early. Occasionally he would play polo on the Marsa ground, where he had been coached by Lord Mountbatten, and in the evenings the Prince and Princess often dined and danced at the Phoenecia Hotel.

One could not overlook, however, the fact that Prince Philip's status in Malta was somewhat incongruous. Ashore, Lieutenant the Duke of Edinburgh took precedence – sometimes a trifle embarrassingly – over his commander-in-chief, yet on board his ship he was referred to simply as 'Number One', and he himself addressed the captain as 'sir'. Philip never used royal status for self-aggrandisement, as was evident while serving in *Chequers*. In the normal course he had sat for the command examination, an officer's entrée to his own quarter-deck. Ostensibly there appeared to be little doubt that he would pass it, yet to general surprise he failed in one subject. At the request of Admiral Sir Arthur J. Powers, the Com-

mander-in-Chief, Lieutenant Parker was asked to convey the
unfortunate news. The examiner, Parker was informed, had
'failed him [Philip] in Torpedo and ASDIC', a subject in which
Prince Philip excelled. The Admiral explained that he had
read the paper and in his opinion Philip had passed. When
Parker reported to Philip, the Prince was extremely annoyed,
not as a result of the failure, but because he had not been
treated in the normal way. He warned that if the naval hierarchy tried 'to fix it, I quit the navy for good'. Philip took the
examination again, with success. In July 1950 he received
promotion to lieutenant-commander, and in September he was
appointed to the frigate *Magpie*, then at Malta. This was his
first and last command.

The anomalous situation in which he had found himself
persisted. On shore his social status overshadowed everyone.
Maybe this explains his reluctance to mix freely when off
duty – a tendency that resulted in adverse criticism, especially
among those who sarcastically referred to *Magpie* as 'Edinburgh's private yacht'. It was an insight to Prince Philip of the
problems of British royalty. To be acknowledged as 'sir' by
much senior officers had its embarrassment yet he would have
been accused of aloofness had he ignored all social events.
Nothing however deterred him from following the example of
both grandfather and uncle; he was determined to make his
ship the best in the fleet. To petty officers at Corsham he had
defined discipline as 'the force which causes a man to play the
part required of him in the organization to which he belongs'.
Philip knew that to command a ship's company he must first
win the confidence of the lower deck. Calling his men together,
he warned them that he would be a martinet but at all times
just. He added humorously that they might be taunted because
they formed the complement of the Duke of Edinburgh's yacht.
'Don't you take it,' he confided. 'Any man who comes before
me on a charge with two black eyes can be sure I'll be on his
side.' Some time later one of his men remarked: 'He made us
work like dogs but he treated us like gentlemen.' 'Dukie'
achieved what he set out to accomplish. In the annual regatta
'Magger's' boat crews won six out of ten events, with Prince

Philip himself stroking one of her boats to victory. Both in manœuvres and sports *Magpie* was established as the cock of the fleet, with a massive plywood rooster fixed jauntily on her single mast. Kurt Hahn's prediction of potential leadership had been confirmed.

Throughout this time, Prince Philip never ignored his honorary posts and commitments in Britain. When in port he could off-load much of the mail on to his secretary, but when afloat he laboured with correspondence in his cabin late into the night.

If Philip ever seriously contemplated that he could be the husband of the heiress presumptive and pursue a full-time naval career, circumstances disillusioned him. Clearly the two did not harmonize. Exacerbating all this was the King's deteriorating health, and consequently the onus of royal duties weighed more heavily on Princess Elizabeth. Furthermore, the government had decided that she and Prince Philip should make a tour of Canada, taking in a short visit to the United States. When Prince Philip was ordered to Britain in July 1951, it was described as indefinite leave. The Navy had occupied more than a third of his life. So far he had known no other career. But he would never return. A new variegated pattern of life awaited him and he anticipated it with a degree of gloom. Sadly bidding goodbye to *Magpie*'s crew, ranked in shining 'whites' in the sunshine of Lazaretto Creek, he said: 'The past eleven months have been the happiest of my sailor life.'

For Princess Elizabeth and Prince Philip, the tour of Canada and the United States in the autumn of 1951 was a testing time and a foretaste of things to come. At first the tour was of modest proportions – visits to three cities in ten days. But it was then augmented into a gruelling 15,000-mile journey, an exhausting programme embracing thirty-five fourteen-hour days. The Edinburghs were to have departed on 25 September in the liner *Empress of Britain*, but suddenly there came the shocking news that King George VI was gravely ill with cancer. The announcement at once threw plans into a state of chaos. Should the tour go ahead or be abandoned? The King himself supplied the answer. Two days before sailing time an affected lung was removed, yet, despite the anxieties and confusion, the King resolutely insisted that the tour should continue.

However, the emergency had unfortunately created what seemed to be an insoluble problem. The time factor prevented a journey by sea and the politicians prevented the heiress presumptive from travelling long distances by plane. Confronted with a bulging schedule, Prince Philip delivered an ultimatum securing one of his earliest victories over officialdom. With the King's connivance he devised a means of forcing the government to allow the Princess to fly or cancel the tour.

Philip succeeded after a meeting with Clement Attlee, then the Prime Minister, and Winston Churchill, the elder statesman, who more than anyone opposed exposing the Princess to danger. Safety conferences at London Airport were insisted upon, but on 8 October Elizabeth and Philip flew to Montreal, the Princess saddened by thoughts of her father and carrying a sealed envelope containing a message to both Houses of Parliament in the event of his death. Thus Princess Elizabeth's unremitting programme was doubly arduous.

The Canadian–U.S. tour was a calculated exercise to train Princess Elizabeth in her development as heiress presumptive without the eclipsing figures of her parents, a strain great enough in normal circumstances. She therefore relied enormously on the solicitous attention of Prince Philip. Tactfully he fulfilled the duties of her protective consort, yet always left her within the direct line of the public spotlight. At all times her husband's reassuring presence was near, there to patch up any flaw in the programme and to charm the crowd and ease her tension with spontaneous wit.

To a lesser degree Prince Philip himself was on trial, but he quickly demonstrated that his gregarious personality was ideal as a consort. From then onwards – right into Elizabeth's reign – Philip would display his extraordinary talent for popularizing the monarch. In North America Princess Elizabeth won the cordiality and affection of the crowds with her graciousness and friendly charm, but it was Philip who adroitly helped her to cast the royal spell over the masses. In the main the Princess had led a sheltered life, away even from the fringe of ordinary people. But life for Prince Philip had been totally different. He was more familiar with its sophistications and a naval career in particular had taught him the language of ordinary people. This enabled him to be more sensitively attuned to the subtleties of public reaction. Thus he was more conscious of the moods of the crowd, meeting them with such self-reliance that an American reporter generously observed: 'Philip could run for Congress on the Republican ticket in Texas and win.' Prince Philip's affability and flexible manner won over both Canadians and Americans. It would be a technique that he would adopt when Princess Elizabeth became Queen. As in the case of the Queen Mother, Prince Philip rightly considers that as the consort, with no specific place in the constitution, he is entitled to a measure of informality in public and to ally it with his ready wit. But in the United States popularity had its drawbacks; at a reception of the British Embassy in Washington the royal couple had to shake hands with some 1,800 guests. Because the White House was undergoing decorations, Princess Elizabeth and Prince Philip stayed with President and Mrs Truman at Blair House. The President took the Princess to meet his aged bedridden mother-in-law in an upper room. Churchill had recently been returned as Prime Minister and Princess Elizabeth was greeted with the remark: 'I am so glad your father has been re-elected.'

The success of Princess Elizabeth and Prince Philip in North America qualified them to embark on a visit to Kenya, Ceylon, Australia and New Zealand.

Already the tour had twice been cancelled due to the King's illness. But on 31 January 1952 – a bitterly cold day – the tired ailing monarch stood bare-headed, waving to Elizabeth and Philip as they flew off to Nairobi. 'Look out for yourselves,' had been the King's last words. Seven days later they would be back in England. On 5 February pleasant weather drew George VI out of doors with his dogs for his favourite pastime – shooting. At 7.30 the next morning, James MacDonald, his assistant valet, found him dead.

To adapt himself to the inescapable fact that his wife was

now Queen Elizabeth II perhaps imposed more demands on Philip's discipline than at any time. He had known that this situation would arise one day but, he had secretly hoped, not so soon. He revealed years later that within the house 'people used to come to me and ask me what to do. In 1952 the whole thing changed, however, very considerably'. He had been 'master of the house' but now it was different. This had been stressed with some abruptness at St James's Palace the day the Queen received the homage of the Privy Council and signed her oath of accession. On retiring with her Court officials, Prince Philip had been debarred from following the Queen until an official was induced to let him pass. This in itself was a presentiment of the future; he must learn to realize that there was no place for him officially in affairs of State. Such matters devolved entirely upon the Queen and the courtiers, jealous of their prerogatives, would ensure that they consulted solely and directly with their sovereign. To Prince Philip's logical mind the situation seemed wholly incongruous. One cannot say whether he spoke plaintively or with some asperity, but he later commented:

'Because she is the sovereign everybody turns to her. If you have a King and Queen, there are certain things people automatically go to the Queen about. But if the Queen is also the *Queen* they go to her about everything. She is asked to do much more than she would normally do, and the fact that they (the household) report to the Queen is important to them, and it is frightfully difficult to persuade them not to go to the Queen, but to come to me.'

On 15 February the body of King George VI was buried in the vaults of St George's Chapel, Windsor. As the coffin vanished slowly through a cavity in the choir floor, Queen Elizabeth II sprinkled it with Windsor soil from a silver bowl. Her gesture symbolized the end of the reign of George the Good and the dawn of the Second Elizabethan Age. The appearance of a young sovereign on the throne stimulated a sense of false euphoria. The name Elizabeth stirred thoughts of

Gloriana. Sir Henry Channon rejoiced in the new reign and welcomed it, later observing: 'There is a new festival spirit about. A young Queen; an old Prime Minister [Churchill] and a brave buoyant Butler budget. Has he put us [Conservatives] in for a generation?' Amid the hysteria everyone seemed to ignore the indisputable fact that national regeneration could only be the outcome of circumstance, moral strength and the unconquerable will of the people. The Queen and her family would set high standards for others to emulate. These can be crystallized in her own keen sense of the proprieties expressed in 1949 while addressing the British Mothers Union. On that occasion, she had stressed:

'Some of the very principles on which the family and there-fore the health of the nation is founded are in danger. We live in an age of growing self-indulgence, of hardening materialism, of falling moral standards. There will always be unhappy marriages, especially when, as in time of war, and of housing shortages, it is difficult for people to live normal married lives. But when we see around us the havoc which has been wrought – above all among children – by the break-up of homes, we can have no doubt that divorce and separation are responsible for some of the darkest evils in our society today.

'I do not think you can perform any finer service than to help maintain the Christian doctrine that the relationship of husband and wife is a permanent one, not to be lightly broken because of difficulties or quarrels. I believe there is a far greater fear in our generation of being labelled priggish. In consequence people are sometimes afraid to show dis-approval of what they know to be wrong, and thus end by seeming to condone what in their hearts they dislike. I am sure that it is just as wrong to err on that side as it is to be intolerant or over critical.'

In turn Prince Philip would also warn of national decline and even degeneration. He focused on what he called 'the pathology of social diseases'; all communities were the result of an empirical advance – 'but the point is that nowadays we are able to build, technically to build, communities, new towns, housing estates – but we don't seem to be able to build them as communities particularly successfully ... this includes the study of disease, partly medical, partly social, which afflicts modern communities ... The problem of the common health ... is really the problem of our times.'

The politicians would chafe under Prince Philip's strictures. ('To understand what Ministers are saying sometimes, you must buy a gobbledegook dictionary and add an arbitrary ten years to every promise they make.') Altogether there would be many spurious claims and the first quarter of a century of the Queen's reign would end in economic decay rather than the expected Utopia.

Greater achievement in that time has been the manner in which Prince Philip has contributed towards enhancing the prospects of the monarchy now and in the coming century. In the process he himself has grown in international stature to a degree unexpected in the early years of the Queen's reign. His status was then very ill-defined and on the surface the prospects seemed extremely unstable. Few could have envisaged his future role. His backers, it has been said with some aptness, had no 'hint of the power-house of energy and ambitions they were plugging into the royal grid'. Finding himself amid the ambience of the British Court, Prince Philip could simply have gratified his personal whims in his new-found haven, appearing in public now and then, sometimes a few discreet steps behind the Queen. But if anyone anticipated this then their expectations were brusquely dismissed. Such a life was out of character with his temperament. Yet at the outset of the Queen's reign Prince Philip had to tread warily, for so far he had not won complete acceptance. As someone advised him: 'To get out of an insane asylum an inmate must prove to the doctors that he is twice as sane as the people outside. In a sense, your case is now being examined by Dr Britain.'

Indeed, from the day of the Queen's accession to her coronation – an interval of sixteen months – Prince Philip had many personal knotty problems to unravel. In the early days, not the least was to acclimatize himself to the official atmosphere at Buckingham Palace. Both Queen Elizabeth and Prince Philip had wished to continue living in the privacy of Clarence House, using Buckingham Palace as the hub of State affairs. Years earlier there had been a parallel arrangement: Buckingham Palace had been purchased as the monarch's residence, St James's Palace remaining as the centre for official business. That is why diplomats in Britain who are accredited to Queen Elizabeth still present their Letters of Credence to the Court of St James although they are today received at Buckingham Palace – usually in the 1844 Room. But Churchill refused to accede; Buckingham Palace was now accepted by tradition as the sovereign's home and must remain so.

It was at Buckingham Palace that Prince Philip received and attended to the requirements of the major guests at the King's funeral. This and the strain of recent months now left their mark and the Prince confided in Alexandria, his cousin, that he felt anaesthetized. The upshot was a bout of yellow jaundice from which he had scarcely recovered when a controversy erupted due to his name.

5

The Family of Mountbatten

Prince Philip had already noted that to be a consort had its anomalies. Prince Bernhard of the Netherlands, whose situation was similar, had advised: 'To succeed as both a husband and a subject, I believe you need a tightrope walker's sense of balance – and an understanding wife.' Prince Philip doubtless had the latter but there was also protocol to contend with. In their marriage, for instance, Queen Elizabeth had promised 'to love cherish and obey' her husband. This meant that she would obey him merely as a wife, but as the Queen she would be the one to require obeisance. Even his presence in the coronation coach was at the Queen's command, not at her invitation. But now a question arose which concerned him deeply. The Government, reinforced by public sentiment, insisted that the name of the Royal Family should revert from Mountbatten to Windsor. There was the insinuation that the ambitious Mountbattens had encroached too far on the monarchy and should be checked.

The Mountbattens, or Battenbergs, have roused so much passionate argument over the years that it is worthwhile probing their lineage. Who are they and how did they come to be so entwined in the life of Britain?

The Mountbatten (or Battenberg) line owed its inception to a mid-nineteenth-century romance at the Tsarist Court involving a 'pure, sweet Polish girl'. It was a misalliance, a contravention of the social standards set by Europe's hierarchy in those times. But from it would result a unique family.

In 1841, the Tsarevitch Alexander Nicolaevitch, eldest son of Tsar Nicholas I, married Princess Marie, the sixteen-year-old daughter of Grand Duke Louis II of Hesse. At Marie's request her brother Prince Alexander, who was one year older and a godson of the Tsar, accompanied her to the Imperial Court. Soon malicious tongues were reviving a rumour that had long been whispered in European Courts. Pinpointing the gap between the ages of Alexander and Marie and their elder brothers, the gossips hinted that the younger children were the offspring of an illicit union – the clandestine liaison between the Grand Duchess and her Chamberlain, Baron Augustus von Grancy. But no one could supply a shred of proof and the Tsar contemptuously remarked: 'We can only hope to be the sons of our fathers whose proud name we bear, but who on earth can prove it?' He therefore ordered 'that all this talk shall stop'.

The excitement and grandeur of the St Petersburg Court appealed to Alexander even though the Empress, a Prussian by birth, did not conceal her dislike for the House of Hesse and by Rhine. The Tsar, in contrast, was more tolerant and generous. In December 1843 he re-christened the Borrisoglebosky 17th Lancers after his godson and appointed him their colonel-in-chief. (The family link would be re-forged years later. Among Earl Mountbatten's possessions, there is a letter written to Queen Louise of Sweden, his sister, by the Emperor's second daughter, the Grand Duchess Tatiana, announcing the Queen's appointment as colonel-in-chief.)

Handsome and physically strong, and endowed with intelligence and a talent for painting, this brilliant, personable young man not unnaturally became involved in amorous sallies. But unfortunately he made the mistake of falling in love with the Tsar's own daughter, the Grand Duchess Olga, whom Nicholas had planned to offer in marriage in a dynastic union. Meanwhile, an attempt was made to cure Alexander's aching heart. An army was being raised to crush a rebellion in the Caucasus, where Shamyl, the tribal leader, now legendary throughout Europe, was trying to free his people from the Tsarist yoke. The Tsarevitch implied to his brother-in-law that his services would be of use to the campaign – in effect, an order to temporarily leave Court. On 6 April 1845 Prince Alexander, who had been given the rank of brigadier-general, wrote plaintively in his diary: 'I do not know whether Olly really loves me. She was little affected when I said good-bye. All she gave me as a farewell was to read every day the 19th Psalm as a memento of her.'

The war was highlighted by shocking brutality, the prisoners of either side being the victims of terrible torture. However, if captured, Alexander was destined for another fate; reports of his philandering had even reached the half-savage Circassians. 'We are terribly depressed,' he wrote to his sister and the Tsarevitch, 'our position is perilous ... we cannot return the way we came and before us lie dark forests full of fanatical foes.' As for himself, 'according to reports of prisoners we have taken, Shamyl's wife has asked her husband to be given the German prince (me) when he is captured'.

Alexander distinguished himself in the fighting, and his trophies of war included Shamyl's Koran and papers which, together with Prince Alexander's pistols, are today in the care of Earl Mountbatten at his Hampshire home.

The news that his beloved Olga was affianced to Charles, heir to King William of Wurtemberg – 'that flabby and insignificant Swabish princeling' – horrified Alexander. By now one notes that independent spirit without which there would have been no Mountbatten line. Writing to his sister from Vienna during 'six months of well-deserved leave', he confided:

'It seems that one should marry to please oneself and not to please other people. I grieve for Olly and I am not at all happy about your suggestions about Vivi [Louise of Mecklemburg-Schwerin]. I am not at all disposed to tie myself down at the age of twenty and three. If I marry her I shall have to stay in Darmstadt with the prospect of doing nothing all the rest of my life or in St Petersburg where I cannot live a married life at all without money. So you will not be surprised if I avoid the trap that is set for me so openly.'

Returning to the Russian Court, Prince Alexander plunged wholeheartedly into a life of dissolution, his extravagances centring on gambling, drunkenness and love-making. Each was carried to such excess that he incurred the Tsar's displeasure.

Money – at least the lack of it – was the Prince's major concern, for the sums that Sasha his brother-in-law could not eke out had now to be met by the money-lenders. Finally mounting debts forced Alexander to resort to more devious means, thus adhering to a practice then widespread at Court; for many received money from clandestine sources or accepted prizes for the occasional discreet service, and in some cases even sold intelligence to some European power.

Prince Alexander allowed himself to be the tool of the financial world. Mayer Amschel Rothschild and his sons had progressed far from their early poverty in Jew Street in the Frankfurt ghetto. From their mansions in London, Paris and other strategic centres, their financial ramifications penetrated far into Europe's corridors of power. There were many Courts and governments over which their shadow fell and at times not a few had good cause to be grateful. Such a person had been that Elector of Hesse-Cassel who, scurrying in 1806 in the van of the all-conquering Bonaparte, relied on the astuteness of old Mayer Amschel to protect his wealth.

Indeed, the Rothschild association with the Grand Dukes of Hesse was long standing. In the circumstances, they not unnaturally looked upon Alexander as the ideal instrument to complete their financial empire – a branch in St Petersburg. Thus the second Mayer Amschel sent to Russia a skilful negotiator – Moses Davidson – who dangled before Alexander riches and a lucrative annuity if he induced the Tsar to receive credits to finance the State budgets and the new railways. But the young soldier was no match for the methodical graft at Court. For many years Stieglitz, the German bankers, had monopolized the major financial dealings in Russia and the Tsar's advisers – the recipients of covert gifts – were determined that they should continue. Their most potent weapon concerned the Russian attitude to Jews who were prohibited by law from permanent residence. Furthermore, no Jewish concern could employ in excess of five clerks.

Prince Alexander's overtures, rousing resentment at Court, proved abortive. St Petersburg would continue to be the only leading centre to ban the Rothschilds. They would be resentful.

Resentment of another kind would have an important bearing on Alexander's future. At a ball in January 1848 the Countess Shuvalov sent the Prince a wrathful note warning him that unless he ceased paying attention to her daughter, Sophie, she would lodge a protest with the Tsar. The bearer of this message was a lady-in-waiting of his sister Marie. Her name was Julie and she was the orphan of a Russian general killed during the Polish rebellion in 1830. With Prince Alexander, she would found the House of Battenberg, or Mountbatten, and Prince Philip, Duke of Edinburgh, would be her great-grandson. Earl Mountbatten, in *The Mountbatten Lineage*, devotes much space to the kings, dukes and other notable progenitors, but not many lines are granted to Julie von Hauke, the female co-founder.

Rather diminutive – a little more than five feet tall – Julie was sometimes known at the Imperial Court as Fraulein von Hauke or Countess von Hauke, but in general she was held to be 'that poor, sweet Polish girl'. Julie, who was twenty-three years old in 1848, would bequeath to her descendants that pronounced nose which would be an aspect of the Mountbatten features. Not a great deal is known of Julie's ancestry. Her great-grandfather had been a tradesman in Mainz, and a son, Johann, had gained some prominence. Attendance at the Latin School secured a clerkship in the State Office of the King of Saxony (who was then King of Poland also) before graduating as secretary to the Governor in Warsaw. When Poland was divided by Russia and Prussia, Johann Hawke – who decided on the more aristocratic Hauke – remained in Warsaw as a Russian official, marrying the daughter of the pastor of Sassenheim, Maria Salome Schweppenhauser. Of their seven children, Moritz, the eldest, received a commission in the Tsar's army. Yet when Poland retrieved independence through Napoleon, he enlisted in the Polish Legion and fought under Bonaparte's flag. When Napoleon's military fortunes waned, however, he returned to Poland, again changing allegiance to take command of a brigade in Tsar Alexander's army.

It was a shrewd move, for in 1820 he rose to more rarefied heights as Minister of War in the Russian-controlled puppet government of Poland. Four years earlier Moritz had married

Sophie Lafontaine, daughter of a French doctor who, with his Hungarian wife, lived at Biberach-on-the-Riss near Lake Constance in Wurtemberg. Moritz was fifteen years older than his wife who bore him three children.

By a stroke of fate, as the War Minister, Moritz and his family resided at the Palais Bruehl where his father had served the Saxony governor in a less august capacity. In 1829 Tsar Nicholas promoted him to the rank of general, adding that he could assume the title of Count. But within a year – in November – Moritz, the Tsarist pawn, lay dead, dying at the hands of revolutionaries while trying to save the life of the Governor-General, Grand Duke Constantine, brother of the Tsar. After witnessing the hacking down of her husband, Countess Sophie Hauke died of a broken heart within a year, and Tsar Nicholas ordered that her orphans should be reared as his wards at Court.

At her own request or not, Julie was separated from her relations, as her daughter Marie would record many years later:

'Mamma's extraction always had about it a halo of romance. Nothing interested me more than to learn something about her relatives, but she never spoke of them herself. As the youngest of her family, brought up in St Petersburg, she had less of the Polish element about her than the rest. Now and then she would mention a member of the Hauke family, and the events of which she told were always shadowed by the tragedy of her nation, for not only her father, but other family members, too, had died violent deaths.'

A portrait painting of Countess Julie depicts her with dark brown hair parted in the middle and adorned with looped pearls. The long straight nose infuses her features with that determination and strength which was to be evident in years to come. Even when she met Alexander it is doubtful if there was an immediate romance, for the Prince's clandestine meetings with Sophie Shuvalov persisted – actually with Julie's aid as trusted confidante. The liaison, however, was discovered and Countess Shuvalov fulfilled her threat; she complained to the Tsar. Prince Alexander was brusquely informed to end the affair or quit the Court. The Tsar wished him to marry his niece, the Grand Duchess Catherine, daughter of his brother Michael (who, incidentally, detested the Hesse prince) and there was the hint that he might be offered a Balkan throne.

One thing is certain: if Alexander had accepted, there would have been no Battenberg line. Circumstances, however, were taking their own course. On his twenty-fifth birthday – on 15 July 1848 – among the love notes that Prince Alexander received was one from Countess Julie. Wrote the Prince: 'I really did not notice that the girl was in love with me.' It was a rude awakening, and one which would leave its imprint on British history. Briefly, Countess Julie became the mistress of Prince Alexander, an intimacy that remained unknown to the Tsar until, during the autumn of 1849, opening a door in the Crown Princess's suite, he saw his ward and Alexander in a passionate embrace. The enraged Emperor threatened to despatch the Prince to a Siberian garrison. Instead, Alexander came under the sadistic persecution of the Grand Duke Michael, commander-in-chief of the Imperial Guard. For Alexander, now in disgrace, life grew intolerable and in August 1850 the Tsar acceded to his request to take indefinite leave. First he visited Darmstadt where, as Louis III, his elder brother now occupied the grand ducal throne. Then for a while he stayed in Paris before moving on to his first experience of London.

Prince Alexander was astonished by 'the liberal ways of life in London' – an impact which (like his descendants) would endear him to Britain. After visiting the offices of *The Times*, he wrote to his sister in St Petersburg: 'It is utterly amazing how the journalists can write quite freely about the Royal Family, even about the private lives of Queen Victoria and her Consort in a newspaper which is being read by everybody.'

Absence from Russia in no way ameliorated the Tsar's anger towards him. Returning to St Petersburg in the early part of 1851, Prince Alexander encountered a frigidity which he found unbearable. The climax arrived when Grand Duke Michael, conspiring to have him banned from the Imperial Court, untruthfully alleged that the Prince's behaviour had 'absolutely demoralised the Officer Corps'. Prince Alexander concluded that the time had come to sever himself from the Imperial Court.

Until now it is difficult to assess the true relationship between Alexander and Countess Julie. Only the previous year, when the betrothal was announced of Sophie Shuvalov and Prince Brobrinsky, Alexander had written dejectedly in his diary: 'I cannot bear the idea of Sophie belonging to someone else.' But now, confiding in Countess Julie that he proposed to quit St Petersburg, he acceded to her request to take her with him. Was the Mountbatten line the result of impulsive action? Whatever the explanation, the outcome of their engagement was explosive. Because Countess Julie was a ward of the Court, Alexander had first to get the Tsar's consent to their marriage. But the Prince must have realized that his request would be denied; he was breaking an inflexible social code by wishing to marry outside his caste. One day Alexander's sister would be the Empress of Russia and to the Court it was unthinkable that her sister-in-law should be her former lady-in-waiting. It was a threat to the autocratic system by which the Tsar and his counsellors exercised power and countered revolution.

Indeed, Marie pleaded and protested, fearing that the romance would undermine her status at Court. From Darmstadt the Grand Duke Louis advised his brother to marry 'one of the girls of that big litter of Catherine the Great'. Sasha warned that should Alexander marry without the Tsar's approval he would be banished from Russia. This was confirmed by the furious Emperor at a formal audience some weeks later. Alexander, however, stubbornly refused to be dissuaded. On 4 October 1851 he left the country of his adoption. So too did Countess Julie von Hauke, both travelling separately until they reached Warsaw. Continuing to Breslau in Prussian Silesia, a priest married them on 28 October. When this became known to the Tsar, Alexander was immediately cashiered from the Imperial Guard. Thus stripped of his rank, he forfeited his pension.

Prince Alexander of Hesse, now twenty-eight, had been deprived of both military rank and money. But more urgent was the problem of Countess Julie's status. Of inferior rank, she could not be accepted as a Princess of Hesse. This was a family knot which Louis III asked his disgruntled Chief Minister, Herr Karl Friedrich von Dalwigk, to unravel when he summoned him on the cheerless night of 3 November 1851. It was raining hard as the Minister's carriage rumbled into the Parade Platz, then along the drive to the sixteenth-century palace. Sitting before the library fire and tortured by gout, Louis testily asked his Minister how they could regularize a ridiculous marriage which had annoyed so many – even the British Queen. Explaining the constitutional aspect, Dalwigk pointed out that Prince Alexander could retain his title and rank and his wife would be raised to the dignity of a Countess of the Grand Duchy of Hesse-Darmstadt and by Rhine. Any children of the union, however, would have to bear the mother's name and be deprived of princely titles.

'But what name?' asked Louis. At first Dalwigk suggested Kellerburg: there was a castle of that name dating from the fifteenth century, but Louis thought it unsuitable. Dalwigk now mentioned a hamlet near Wiesbaden named after an ancient knightly family which had participated in the Crusades. Since the family had died out in the fourteenth century, the title was defunct but it could be revived.

'They were the Counts von Battenberg, Your Highness,' Dalwigk explained. 'They had a fine castle overlooking the River Eder at Battenberg. The round tower and bastion still stand on the eastern heights of the Westerwald.'

Two days later a decree announced that His Illustrious Highness the Grand Duke Louis III of Hesse-Darmstadt and by Rhine had graciously elevated on this fifth day of November in the year of Our Lord 1851 Fraulein Julie Teresa von Hauke, daughter of Count Moritz von Hauke, deceased, and Countess von Hauke, née Mademoiselle Sophie de Lafontaine, to the rank, dignity and title of a Countess von Battenberg, and that the issue of the morganatic marriage of His Highness the Prince Alexander Ludwig Georg Emil of Hesse-Darmstadt and by Rhine, third son of the late lamented Grand Duke Louis II,

and the said Countess von Battenberg would for ever enjoy
the rank, dignity and title of Counts and Countesses von Battenberg, but would have no rights or claim to the succession to
the throne in accordance with the Act of Constitution of
1820.

Dalwigk wrote to Alexander acquainting him that, for political reasons, his presence in Darmstadt would be an embarrassment. The Prince therefore took his newly-acquired wife to
Geneva, living in a small private hotel until sister Marie and
brother Louis gave the monetary aid that enabled them to
rent a villa. There, the first child Marie was born. More help
was forthcoming. Dalwigk had advised Prince Alexander to
seek service with his young cousin, the Emperor Francis Joseph
of Austria, and through the mediation of the Tsarevitch, the
Tsar placed Alexander on the retired list as a major-general.
But it was not until the following October that Francis Joseph
appointed him garrison commander at Graz. Military duties
were not onerous and to counter tedium Alexander and Julie,
together with local dignitaries, dabbled in occultism at the castle
of Graz. More important to British history is the fact that Louis,
their eldest son, was born on 24 May 1854. One day he would
be the eminent First Sea Lord in the Royal Navy, the father
of Earl Mountbatten of Burma and the grandfather of Prince
Philip, Duke of Edinburgh.

For the next eight years Prince Alexander served the Austrian
monarchy with distinction, commanding a division of the army
of occupation at Verona in northern Italy, where another son
Alexander was born in 1857 to be followed the next year by a
third, Henry, when he was transferred to Milan. In 1858, while
commanding the Milan garrison Prince Alexander witnessed
the riots in Italy and the growth of the secret societies of Garibaldi, and in the following year he commanded an Austrian in-
fantry division in the brief war against a resurgent Italy aided
by the French. Alexander fought in two fierce battles – Magenta
and Solferina – and at the latter led a battalion of Imperial
Guards in a bayonet charge and prevented a rout. In 1861 a
grateful Emperor promoted him to lieutenant-general and
awarded him the rare Order of Maria Theresa. The same year

saw the birth of Francis Joseph, his youngest son, in Padua. In the following year he retired and returned with his family to Hesse.

After his banishment from Russia, Prince Alexander grew in political stature, especially when Sasha succeeded to the Tsarist throne as Alexander II. Prince Alexander was the confidant of kings and sometimes the intermediary in the political machinations of Russia, Austria and France. For these subtle assignments he had chosen the perfect wife, for Countess Julie was seen to have a natural flair for political intrigue. Her letters to her sister Sophie testified that Alexander sought and valued his wife's shrewd guidance. Countess Julie von Battenberg could never be criticized for neglecting her husband's ambitions. Whether her maternal instinct was so pronounced is doubtful. In her memoirs, her daughter Marie revealed that, during the family's stay in Austria and the Italian provinces, 'I did not remember much of my parents in these years.' She recalled:

'We children lived entirely to ourselves with Adele and our maid, who at first was old Evi, and later a Swiss girl named Hortense, and then Harriet, an Englishwoman. We saw Papa nearly always in uniform or on horseback. He was the sunshine in our lives ... of Mamma we always stood a little in awe, because she was strict and made us speak French with her. She probably loved us all alike, but it was not her habit to be tender ... and I remember how we elder ones would sometimes comment upon this among ourselves. Praise from her always made a great impression on us ... Next to my father, the one I loved best was Adele Bassing, whose influence extended itself to all my brothers ... To her I owe almost everything that made in the days of my youth for the training of my heart and intellect.'

For years Countess Julie patiently endured humiliation due to her inferior rank, such as the time in November 1856 when the Emperor Francis Joseph and Empress Elizabeth visited Verona. Irritated by Prince Alexander's Russian sympathies, the Emperor foolishly instructed that the Countess von Battenberg should be placed with 'the ladies with lower birth' while her husband stood elsewhere as a prince of royal blood. He went further; Julie was deliberately ignored as she curtsied. Nor could she ever accompany Alexander to St Petersburg. Memories at Court were much too long, even after the Grand Duke Louis III elevated her to royalty as the Princess of Battenberg at Christmas 1858, thereby entitling her children and descendants to be known as Prince and Princess of the House of Battenberg with the embellishment of 'Durchlaucht', or Serene Highness.

Prince Alexander and his family settled in the Alexander Palace, an attractive rococo mansion on the Luisenplatz in Darmstadt (which would render public service in modern times as a central post office). In summer they would move to the twin-towered castle of Heiligenberg, standing in a wooded valley beneath a pine-clad mountain. As far as is known, only one of Princess Julie's relatives ever visited Heiligenberg. This was Alexander de Hauke, a Polish patriot who was exiled by the Tsar. After studying at Heidelberg University, he returned to Poland in 1863, participated in the anti-Tsarist revolution and is presumed to have been killed. This hostility to the Tsar by members of the Hauke family embarrassed Prince Alexander of Hesse. A member of the Haukes fought against the Russian army and others rebelled against the ruling regime in other European countries. Count Joseph von Hauke, one of Princess Julie's nephews, even discarded the family name. Preferring to be nicknamed Boszak (Barefoot), he died fighting beside Garibaldi in 1867 at the Battle of Giacomo.

Alexander, however, was more concerned with the Hesse branch of the family. His nephew Prince Louis of Hesse, who would succeed Alexander's childless brother as Grand Duke, was betrothed to Princess Alice, the second daughter of Queen Victoria. The English connection had prompted Prince Alexander to consider journeying to England to renew his contact with the Rothschilds and enter business, but at the Tsar's request he remained in Germany. Count Otto von Bismarck, who sought German unification and regarded Austria as an obstacle, was trying to effect greater collaboration between Prussia and

Russia. The Tsar wished to be secretly informed of the latest developments.

Bismarck would actually obtrude into Alexander's life and be a stumbling-block to his aspirations. When King Otto fled from Greece, Count Rechberg, the Austrian Foreign Minister, wrote to Prince Alexander seeking his candidature for the vacant throne. The offer had the backing of Napoleon III, the Tsar and the British Government, but Bismarck, as Chancellor of Prussia, vetoed it because of Alexander's Austrian and Russian interests. If the Prince had worn the Greek crown Battenberg history would inevitably have taken a different course. There would certainly have been no Prince Philip of Greece.

This was the second throne that eluded Alexander. In 1857 Sasha had remarked that he would 'look for a crown' for him 'perhaps as the ruler of a new Rumania'. Nothing ever transpired, but three decades hence, Alexander would witness the son who bore his christian name mount the throne in neighbouring Bulgaria. (In 1870 Napoleon III would submit Alexander's candidature for the Spanish throne, but the Tsar and the British and Austrian Governments refused to unite with France against Bismarck.)

Annoyed with the British Government for having ceded so easily to Bismarck, a sympathetic Queen Victoria welcomed Alexander to Britain, a visit which coincided with the christening at Windsor Castle on 5 April 1863 of the daughter of his nephew Louis and Princess Alice. One day the Queen-Empress's little granddaughter would marry his son, Prince Louis, and become the first Marchioness of Milford Haven, and Prince Philip's grandmother.

From that particular time a Battenberg (or Mountbatten) would in varying degrees contribute to the story of the British Crown, and more so when Prince Alexander's younger son, Henry, married Queen Victoria's youngest daughter Beatrice. Indeed, Henry, as the sovereign's companion and adviser, would enjoy the Queen's closest confidence. A rapport already thrived between Prince Alexander and the Prince of Wales (the future Edward VII) – who, to Alexander's eyes was 'a funny little man. His features are not bad, he is a male edition of his sister Alice, but he is so broad for his height that he looks shorter than his wife'. Any of Alexander's descendants who sought seats of power need only reflect on the example set by their male progenitor for inspiration. In London, there were meetings with Lord Palmerston and Lord John Russell, his Foreign Secretary, and Alexander, ever faithful to the Tsar, would write that the British statesmen 'treat me as a colleague, they are well-informed through their secret agents about some of the negotiations I have conducted with Napoleon and Francis Joseph'.

In retirement he saw much of Heiligenberg. Here, periodically the Battenberg children, whom the German Kaiser hailed as the most handsome family in Europe, would welcome their contemporaries from the Courts of St Petersburg, London and Berlin. It was a gathering of Europe's houses of power.

Despite Prince Alexander's abortive aspirations to occupy a European throne, he had created a solid social foundation for his descendants. As one writer has neatly expressed:

'The thin blood of the Hesse princes received many renascent transfusions: German and Polish, French and English, Greek and Hungarian, Jewish and Spanish. The Battenbergs and the Mountbattens have come a long way. In pursuit of their family interest they either allied themselves with, or fought, the Tsars and the Kaisers, the Emperors of France and Austria, Bismarck and the Sultan, gave a ruler to Bulgaria, queens to Spain and Sweden, a princess to Greece, a husband to a prima donna, two First Sea Lords to Britain, a Viceroy of India and a husband to the granddaughter of a Jewish financier, a salesman to a New York store, a wife to a London decorator – and, of course, the present Heir to the Throne of English kings.'

The Battenberg–Mountbatten relationship with Europe's other royal houses should not be minimized, but it was the links by marriage to Queen Victoria's descendants that stabilized and nurtured their status in modern times. Prince Louis of Battenberg, for instance, married a grand-daughter of the Queen-Empress. His brother Henry was wed to her youngest daughter. Marriage through Prince Philip would finally join the Mountbattens inextricably with the reigning house. Just as Prince Henry had been a confidant and adviser of Queen Victoria, so had Prince Louis been the intimate of King George V. His son, Earl Mountbatten of Burma, would enjoy the closest friendship with Edward VIII and George VI. But Prince Louis's grandson would transcend all by becoming the Consort of the British Queen. In the last century and a quarter since the Battenberg–Mountbatten line was founded, its members have etched their personalities on their times. Coming to more recent years, Clement Attlee, as Britain's Labour Prime Minister, is reputed to have said: 'It's a funny thing, those Mountbattens are the only members of the Royal Family who have ever shown great ability. All three of them – Prince Louis, a great sailor who was done in by the *Globe* in 1914; Dickie (Lord Mountbatten), who became Chief of the Defence Staff in spite of being royal, not because of it; and Philip, I think, if he had a chance.'

In one sense Attlee's words were inaccurate and ill-chosen, for the Royal Family has produced sovereigns who have displayed diplomatic skill, with the right degree of tact and aplomb, in their onerous duties. Over the years tact has not always been one of the Mountbattens' more conspicuous traits. In consequence, at times they have been the centre of controversy and criticism. But beyond dispute is their intelligence, courage and abilities which are manifestly above those of the ordinary. The Mountbattens have been described as Britain's most outstanding family. It could be argued that this is hyperbole but, exaggeration or not, one can conjure to mind few families in which successive generations have made such an incisive impact on British affairs. Prince Louis, for instance, who founded that part of the line which is now completely British, was the First Sea Lord through whose sagacity the Royal Navy attained its utmost efficiency and preparedness in the First World War. In confirmation Winston Churchill wrote: 'So much of my work in endeavouring to prepare the Fleet for war was dependent on the guidance and help I received from Prince Louis of Battenberg ... He had a far wider knowledge of war by land and sea, and of the Continent of Europe, than most of the other Admirals I have known.' Prince Louis was in a sense more English than the English, yet he could not escape the vituperative attack because of the hysteria and hatred of anything Germanic in the First World War. As a result, quite wrongly Prince Philip's grandfather was accused of faulty dispositions – if not treachery – when cruisers were torpedoed in the North Sea and Craddock's fleet was lost at Coronel. Worst of all his name was German. Thus the name Battenberg was anglicized to Mountbatten and King George v created him the first Marquess of Milford Haven.

In turn, Earl Mountbatten of Burma, who was born at Windsor Castle and is a great-grandson of Queen Victoria, has at times roused dislike by what appears to be a disregard for public reaction. (Some would say that Prince Philip has copied this avuncular trait.) For instance, not even the combined fury of the pundits of both the Air Ministry and the Admiralty dissuaded him from his resolve to unify Britain's defences. And nothing deterred him when, as the last Viceroy of India, he presided over what has been dubbed the dissolution of the Empire, thus invoking Tory wrath. Similarly, his nephew Prince Philip, the progenitor of Britain's future sovereigns, has sometimes found himself in the midst of dispute. One notable instance was that of his name.

Like any woman in the land, by her marriage to Philip Mountbatten in 1947 Princess Elizabeth changed her name to that of her husband. Therefore, when as Queen Elizabeth II she acceded to the throne, many speculated on whether she would be the last monarch of the House of Windsor. Normally the death of a queen regnant would end her dynasty. Thus, would the Queen's successor, Prince Charles, assume his father's name and found the House of Mountbatten? The topic was debated in learned quarters.

At the time of the birth of the Queen's father, the Royal Family had used no surname since the days of Queen Anne, the last of the reigning Stuarts; for when her successor, the German princeling who became George I, arrived in London from

Hanover he brought no surname. Many years earlier his family
had been known variously as Guelph, Este or Wettin, but for
generations these had been dispensed with. Until 1917 all members of the Royal Family were styled 'Highness'. However,
during that year King George v restricted the use of princely
styles to children of the monarch and of the monarch's sons
but not of his daughters. It was therefore imperative to adopt
a surname for the latter. As Britain was then at war with
Germany, the King decided against continuing Prince Albert's
family name – Saxe-Coburg-Gotha – and coined the name of
Windsor for Queen Victoria's descendants in the male line.
It was the desire of the Queen's grandfather that the name
would be permanent: 'Determined that henceforth our House
and Family shall be styled and known as the House of Windsor.'
What he did not anticipate was that the succession might pass
to a female.

Here there was precedent. Queen Anne was the last Stuart,
Queen Victoria the last Hanoverian. Yet on the death of
Queen Victoria, the House of Hanover ceased to exist and her
heir, having inherited her father's name, introduced the House
of Coburg. Similarly Queen Elizabeth II succeeded as the last
monarch of the House of Windsor and the first of the Family
of Mountbatten. Conforming to the pattern of the past, when
Prince Charles ascended the throne, he would initiate the House
of Mountbatten.

That appeared to be the situation during the first two months
of the Queen's reign. The surname of the Royal Family was
Mountbatten – a name ranking in the thousand-year-old story
of British monarchs with the Plantagenets, Tudors, Stuarts and
Hanoverians. Yet on 9 April 1952, the *London Gazette* announced: 'The Queen today declared in Council Her Will and
Pleasure that She and Her Children shall be styled and known
as the House and Family of Windsor, and that Her descendants,
other than female descendants who marry, and their descendants
shall bear the name of Windsor.'

It would have been unwise to have renounced the dynastic
name of Windsor. In the people's minds it symbolized the
stability which George v and George vi had ingrained into

national life. Moreover, it was a name which evoked a millennium of British history. But some people were incensed because Prince Philip's name seemed suddenly to have dissolved from the royal pedigree. Their attitude was crystallized in the contention of Mr Dermot Morrah, Arundel Herald of Arms Extraordinary, that the ruling 'did less than justice' to Her Majesty's husband 'as the progenitor of the dynasty to come'. It is suspected that the Queen yielded to the deletion only under pressure. Writing in the *Law Journal* in March 1960, Edward S. Iwi, the constitutional lawyer, contended: 'This (the Family of Mountbatten) continued for only two months because, it is said, as a result of great pressure by Sir Winston Churchill a change was made.' It must have been to the Queen's satisfaction, therefore, that on 30 September 1952, the *London Gazette* again announced: 'The Queen has been graciously pleased by Warrant bearing date the 18th instant to declare and ordain that His Royal Highness Philip Duke of Edinburgh ... shall henceforth upon all occasions ... except where otherwise provided by Act of Parliament have, hold and enjoy Place, Pre-eminence and Precedence next to Her Majesty.'

Prince Philip was now the First Gentleman of the Realm. But more was to come. On 8 February 1960, eleven days before the birth of the Queen's third child – the son to be christened Prince Andrew after Prince Philip's father – the Queen reversed the decision taken eight years earlier. She declared in Council that 'while I and my children shall continue to be styled and known as the House and Family of Windsor, my descendants, other than descendants enjoying the style, title or attributes of Royal Highness and the titular dignity of Prince or Princess, and female descendants who marry and their descendants shall bear the name Mountbatten-Windsor.'

Many citizens were perplexed but a Buckingham Palace official commented succinctly: 'The Queen has always wanted to associate her husband with their descendants. She has had this in mind for a long time and it is close to her heart.'

Some cynics argued that the latest declaration would amount to very little since princes and princesses did not use surnames.

But constitutional lawyers held that they possessed a 'latent' surname. It was generally believed, however, that there could be no Mountbatten-Windsor until the third generation from the monarch. To illustrate this point, it was claimed that if Prince Charles married and a year later had a son, and the latter in due course had two sons, the second grandson of Prince Charles would be the first Hon. Mountbatten-Windsor. The proposal to reintroduce the name Mountbatten was, in the main, severely criticized by the British press. The *Daily Telegraph* claimed that 'it was the normal practice of the Queen's subjects that a child uses the name of his father's family, and this personal wish, natural in an expectant mother, had become stronger than ever'. Some other newspapers, however, were far less charitable. Referring, for instance, to the declaration as a 'curious decision', the *Daily Mirror* questioned: 'Is the decision prudent? If it is prudent, is it necessary? If it is necessary, is it well timed?' pointing out that 'it is only fifteen years after the Second World War against Germany that the British nation are abruptly informed that the name Mountbatten, formerly Battenberg, is to be joined willy-nilly with the name of Windsor.' Some newspapers insinuated that it was not so much the Queen's idea as the dark intrigue of the wicked uncle, Earl Mountbatten of Burma, who was possessed with an almost fanatical desire to perpetuate and exalt his name. The *Daily Mirror* questioned if the Prime Minister and the Cabinet 'were merely informed, or did they agree?' – then dispensing with innuendo forthrightly claimed that 'Earl Mountbatten was fully aware of what was going on'. In the *Daily Mail* one read that the Queen's declaration 'which will hyphenate the newly-forged Mountbatten name indissolubly with the British Crown, can have brought profounder gratification to no one more than Earl Mountbatten, son of Prince Louis of Battenberg, whose name did not ring sweetly in British ears, and uncle of Prince Philip ... certainly the most controversial figure in this forcefully successful family'.

Lord Beaverbrook, that crusader of Empire, who had condemned Earl Mountbatten for what he considered to be the dissolution of the Empire, made no attempt to conceal his virulence. Published the *Daily Express*:

'While he sat in his office in Whitehall and pondered the problems of defence, or the Navy, or whatever high position he happened to be holding, one spectre has always confronted Earl Mountbatten of Burma: that his family name should finally die out. For he himself has two daughters now both married ... and he has a nephew who is the Marquess of Milford Haven. And another who holds perhaps the greater honour and responsibility than any other member of his ancient family – Prince Philip. Small wonder then that Lord Mountbatten, whose devotion to his heritage is little short of fanatical, has for many years nursed a secret ambition that one day, the name of the ruling house of Britain might be Mountbatten ... Within the conclave of the family, Lord Mountbatten has raised the matter more than once: suggested that even if the name of Windsor be retained, the name of Mountbatten might also be included.

'Prince Philip was less concerned than his uncle in the future of the name, though he took pains to see that the Prince of Wales should know of his heritage. He sent over to German genealogists to secure a complete family tree for Prince Charles to see. Through all this, the Queen remained steadfast in one respect. She could never see the name of Windsor, chosen by her grandfather, abandoned by the royal house. On the other hand, she sympathizes with her husband's feelings – and more particularly with the overtures of his uncle. So, the compromise. Her descendants – though not those who stand in direct line to the Throne – shall carry the name Mountbatten-Windsor.'

However, the Beaverbrook Press was mistaken. Thirteen years later, at her wedding at Westminster Abbey on 14 November 1973, the only daughter of Queen Elizabeth and Prince Philip signed her name in the register 'Anne Mountbatten-Windsor'. In the case of Prince Philip, it is claimed that, if there was to be a change, he would have preferred the name

Prince Philip

of Edinburgh to Mountbatten. As for Earl Mountbatten, one cannot say whether he had any influence in combining the name Mountbatten with that of Windsor. But as regards his own title, long before the Queen's announcement in February 1960, he had already taken the precaution to ensure that his earldom, viscountcy and barony should persist. A 'Special Remainder' was incorporated into his Letter Patent whereby 'in default of heirs male of his body', his title should go 'to his elder daughter and the heirs male of her body, and to every other daughter successively in order of seniority of age and priority of birth, and to the heirs male of their bodies'.

6

That Difficult Interregnum

The dispute over the naming of the dynasty was merely one of many irritations in the post-accession period. But Prince Philip has always relished challenge and did not shun the problems of this difficult interregnum. When, for example, his valet wished to resign his duties because he found the Palace formalities too tiresome, he philosophically advised him: 'It affects us all, this new life, but we should at least give it a fair trial.' In his own case he complied with the wishes of the more sober Palace advisers, occasionally creating a sharp tremor by delivering speeches imbued with his own brand of wit. Momentarily this was frowned upon, for among his sons King George v had emphatically banned humour in public speaking and the ruling had stuck. Philip took part in the round of official visits and engaged in princely sports. But all the time it was imperative to curb his natural exuberance, and never appear to eclipse the Queen.

Sympathetically, to absorb some of the preponderance of energy, the Queen appointed him chairman of the Coronation Commission. This appealed to him. The office teemed with problems such as the tracking down of the ingredients of the oil used in the anointing, the most solemn act of the crowning. Since biblical times the consecration of kings and queens with oil has been a moment of supreme spiritual significance. At one point, however, it seemed that the coronation of Queen Elizabeth II would be deprived of the sacred oil. Unfortunately the last phial had been irretrievably lost among the debris when Nazi bombs fell on Westminster Abbey in 1941.

Inquiries yielded the names of two pharmacists who had compounded the honey-coloured oil for the Queen's father. One had moved to Toronto, but both were now dead. Yet luckily the firm that they had founded still survived; moreover, the new owners had retained the formula which dated from the time of Charles II. Regrettably, however, a piece of information was still missing: the basic oil to be used was unknown. By tracking down the relatives of the one-time royal chemists, there emerged enlightening news: a director had included among his mementoes a small quantity of the oil which had once been exhibited in a chemist's shop. This led to the discovery of the phial in the possession of an elderly lady living in Surrey.

For a time in this early phase of the Queen's reign, Prince Philip is believed to have required strong self-discipline to cope with the negative effects of frustration. In public he was the discreet and deferential consort, always willing to give aid and ease a difficulty with a witty aside. But to one who was self-sufficient, whose nimble mind bubbled with ideas, the prospect of a life of self-effacement was daunting. Secretly he jibbed at the protocol with which he was expected to comply. No one was more sympathetic than the Queen, who devised outlets for his restless energy. First she appointed him Chief Ranger of Windsor Great Park, and empowered him to introduce with his typical thoroughness schemes to reorganize and modernize the royal estates. He applied the same technique – as far as this was feasible – at Buckingham Palace, but these domestic chores and the official engagements were not enough to offset boredom. Maybe to ease the nervous tension he was seen more frequently at social events and visited his sisters in Germany, with whom he had close ties. In the post-war years Prince Philip had been dismayed by their plight. Newspaper reports had described how they had queued at the food rationing offices for meagre allocations, yet he had been helpless to alleviate their hardships. However, if one writer is correct, he compensated for this unavoidable neglect in due course, for 'whenever any of them came to London, they always found an envelope beside their bed filled with pocket money from Philip'.

Speech-making formed another outlet for excessive energy, and it was at this period that he made some of his most cogent remarks. It seemed that he had at last found a niche for himself as the national conscience, encouraging here and perhaps prodding a little forcefully there. Although there was nothing in the constitution to enforce his contentions, he had the freedom to be heard. Some of his earliest speeches were well spiced with warning and we can appreciate their significance more so today. For instance, in 1952, addressing the Chamber of Commerce and Manufacturers in Edinburgh, he appealed for enterprise, enthusiasm, and hard work and went on:

'America has invented the phrase Yes-men for those who flatter great executives. In England we are more troubled by No-men who make it their business to employ clever ignorance in opposing and sabotaging every scheme suggested by those who have energy, imagination and enterprise. I am afraid our No-men are a thousand times more harmful than the American Yes-men. If we are to recover prosperity we shall have to find ways of emancipating energy and enterprise from the frustrating control of constitutionally timid ignoramuses. There is a school of thought [he persisted] which says "What was good enough for my father is good enough for me." I have no quarrel with this sentiment at all, so long as it is not made an excuse for stagnation, frustration and inefficiency, and I am quite sure our fathers would be the first to agree with this. The great name of British commerce was founded on honesty, fair dealing and hard work. But do not forget that the great position of British industry was won when we led the world in inventive imagination and the spirit of adventure.'

But Prince Philip went ignored. Reflecting on the past twenty-five years of the Queen's reign, the Second Elizabethan Age has grown increasingly decadent. One searches for the Raleighs and the Drakes of the new Britain but finds instead the pop star, the drug pusher and the abortionist, as well as the purveyors of porn. Before an inarticulate Church the Second Elizabethan Age has drifted into the Permissive Age and immoral decline. The simple fact is that any suggestion of Gloriana was a foolish dream from the outset. Modern monarchy can merely suggest; it cannot enforce. It can set an example; it cannot compel the nation to emulate. The destiny of a nation – and its success or failure – lies essentially in the intrinsic qualities of the people and the calibre of its political leadership.

To help mitigate frustration, Prince Philip learnt how to pilot aircraft. 'I wanted to fly,' he subsequently revealed, 'like small boys who want to drive railway engines.' On another occasion he explained that he enjoyed the 'intellectual challenge of it all'. What is not generally known is that if the choice had been left entirely to himself, he would have embarked on a career in the Royal Air Force and not the Royal Navy. His rank as Consort demanded that ultimately he must accept the courtesy titles of Admiral of the Fleet, Field Marshal, and a Marshal of the Royal Air Force. To accept the latter without possessing a pilot's licence was repugnant to him. The Establishment, however, did not favour the Prince taking to the air. Winston Churchill hesitated before giving his approval, knowing that if an accident befell Prince Philip he and his government would be severely censured. But he greatly admired the adventurous spirit in the Queen's Consort, and there was precedent. As a prince, George VI had qualified as a pilot without flying solo, but though an instructor had accompanied him, he had never touched the controls. The future Edward VIII had progressed one step further, actually flying solo at Northolt.

There was keen rivalry between the Royal Navy and the Royal Air Force to train the Prince, yet he chose the latter, attending the normal RAF medical test at the central medical establishment in Hallam Street, London, in October 1952. Flight-Lieutenant Carol Gordon, a Meteor instructor at the RAF's Central Flying School, learnt that he had been selected to train the Prince. 'If you kill him,' warned his commanding officer, 'you realize what it will do to the Queen.' When Gordon arrived on 20 October at the headquarters of Home Command, the warning was again echoed by an Air Marshal, two Air Vice-Marshals and an Air Commodore. As if this was not enough, Lord de L'Isle and Dudley, the Secretary of State for Air, speaking for the government, stressed the need for the utmost safety.

Prince Philip, beginning his training in a Chipmunk at White Waltham on 12 November, was determined to fly before Christmas, and in fact made his first solo flight on 20 December. Sometimes he would take off from Smith's Lawn in Windsor Great Park, where a wind-sock had been set up and the cricket pavilion improvised into a briefing room. Because it was close to Sandringham, the next phase of training occurred at Bircham Newton. Philip was not satisfied with just learning to fly, and made a working model of an aircraft with swept wings which he demonstrated to Gordon at Sandringham. Incidentally, although it has now been superseded by a more up-to-date device, he devised an instrument to aid the making of a landing approach. In mid-February he transferred to the more advanced Harvard trainers. In a ceremony at Buckingham Palace two months later – on 4 May 1953 – the royal pilot received his wings.

In the morning at White Waltham, Philip endured the ordeal of demonstrating his latest skill to the press, the news reels and the TV cameras, each no doubt waiting to record the slightest hitch. But the flight was flawless. Indeed, he had learned to fly despite exasperating delays caused by excessive precautions. Summarizing the situation in his diary in April 1953, Gordon wrote:

'When we finished the c-in-c was in the office to apologize to HRH for certain extraordinary contradictions that have taken place recently. Firstly, permission has been refused to transfer to the Oxford (after training on the Harvard) until the Chief of Air Staff has consulted the PM. Second, night flying may not be done until the same procedure has been gone through. HRH has now been flying for six months and during all this time it has been known that night flying and Oxford flying were to be done, and it therefore seems incredible to him that at the last minute an objection is lodged ... the problem seems to be that nobody is willing to take the responsibility ... in their anxiety to see that no harm comes to HRH the whole of his training can be brought to a halt. HRH explained his views in no uncertain terms to the C-in-C, and there is now hope that in future these delays will cease. As far as I can see, the only person who can get any action at all, and who appears to know what is wanted, is HRH, and whenever I am in serious difficulty I tell him.'

Unknown to the Establishment, Philip and Gordon sometimes ignored the rules, for the instructor once recorded that the Prince 'could not stay late, nor fly tonight, because it is the Queen's birthday, so we confined ourselves to three-quarters of an hour instrument flying, followed by an hour solo, during which he went off to practise aerobatics. I told him that the C-in-C wished him to do no more of these for safety's sake, but on such a glorious summer's day if he had just a few and I didn't see him, nobody would know.'

In tribute to his instructor for the anxieties he had sometimes endured, Prince Philip presented Gordon with a silver locket, engraved 'A reward for diligence', with the date of the first solo flight. Gordon, he said, could use it 'to keep pills in'.

Philip received his wings a month before the Queen received her crown. Some days before the coronation, the Prince's private secretary was asked to visit 10 Downing Street and heard Churchill rasp: 'Is it your intention to wipe out the Royal Family in the shortest possible time?' Reports had reached him that Philip had flown in helicopters. This the Prince had found essential in order to visit Commonwealth and Colonial troops at Pirbright and Woolwich and fulfil his coronation commitments as well. Prince Philip won the latest little skirmish with officialdom and established precedent for other members of the Royal Family to follow. So far he had merely flown as a passenger, but in 1956 he qualified as a helicopter pilot with 705 Squadron (Helicopters Royal Navy), and a year later secured more wings with the Army Air Corps at Middle Wallop. When, however, it was announced that he would graduate from piston-engine planes to jets, some people argued that it was now opportune to check Philip's enthusiasm. The *Daily Telegraph* questioned: 'How far are the irreplaceable leaders of a nation justified in taking avoidable risks? For a conflict arises at some stage between the proper desire of a leader to set up an example and his duty in a hazard of life which is precious no less to the nation than to the Queen.' No matter how well intentioned were such counsels, Prince Philip ignored them. Gordon again took his royal pupil aloft, this time in a Meteor VII. Fears were assuaged when it was announced that Flight-Lieutenant C. C. Blount, a Cranwell instructor, would accompany him as a royal equerry.

Prince Philip viewed these inordinate precautions with some annoyance. As a naval officer, he had received no special attention and he did not expect any now. Furthermore, he firmly believed that his call sign 'Rainbow' should be treated in airport control towers in the normal way, and chafed over the system of 'purple airways' which, devised by the Air Ministry, maintains a rigid control along the air corridors used by royal aircraft. Philip wished to avoid inconvenience to others and was justifiably furious when a national newspaper published that members of Reading Flying Club complained that the Duke of Edinburgh spoilt their Saturday morning sport. Prince Philip had visited White Waltham to practise flying a Turbulent plane and, unknown to himself, an order had been issued to ground all planes at Woodley airfield, the Reading Club's headquarters. Philip was totally unaware of the man and said so, a letter from Buckingham Palace adding: 'His Royal Highness would like you to know that if you think you have difficulties getting into the air, they are nothing to what he has to go through.' Good relations were cemented when the Prince accepted honorary membership, one of the few private flying clubs to receive that distinction.

The Prince's stubbornness in not yielding to tedious precautions has resulted in aircraft being accepted as a normal means of travel for royalty. As a pilot with an accumulation of technical knowledge, he could now speak with some authority and without pretension.

That was the attitude which induced him to acquire skill as a pilot of sailplanes before he inaugurated the National Gliding

Championship in 1957. Even though he was a Marshal of the Royal Air Force and a qualified jet pilot, who had been patron of the British Gliding Association for two years, he had never yet experienced the thrill of powerless flight. For the Prince this was an omission which had to be put right. Thus on a gusty afternoon in May of that year, he climbed into the forward seat of a T42 Slingsby glider on an airfield in the Gloucestershire hills. In the rear seat Peter Collier, the resident instructor of the Bristol Gliding Club, explained the controls before take-off. At two thousand feet Collier allowed Prince Philip to take over for a trial flight of some ten minutes. But it sufficed to enable the Prince to pilot a Slingsby Eagle from take-off to touchdown at the championships at Lasham two months later. Congratulating the competitors on their self-sufficiency, Prince Philip commented: 'Sport, pastime, amusement, whatever you like to call it, if more people were similarly sensible and responsible, we wouldn't need so much government.'

An exciting display of naval glider aerobatics – brilliant loops and chandelles – at Mowrs six months earlier, on the eve of the Melbourne Olympic Games, had sparked off his determination to pilot sailplanes. 'It looks great fun,' he said enthusiastically. 'I'd like to try that when I get home.'

When Philip was invited to open the Games in the autumn of 1956, an imaginative idea developed in his fertile mind. Long afterwards he wrote that it soon became apparent 'that there were a good many island communities and outposts in the Indian Ocean, the South Pacific, the Antarctic and the Atlantic which cannot be visited by air, and are too remote and small to get into the usual tours. Although it meant being away for four months, including Christmas and the New Year, I tried to arrange a journey out to Australia and back in the royal yacht *Britannia*.' Actually the Prince and his entourage flew to Mombasa and there joined the yacht.

Prince Philip's Commonwealth tour would take him round the world, journeying some 40,000 miles in 145 days. As he had proposed, there was great emphasis on isolated communities whose chance of welcoming a member of the Royal

Family was singularly remote. To mention a few, there were St Helena and Ascension Island, Gough Island and the Falklands. From the latter he journeyed to Britain's research bases in Antarctica. As reflected by the following extract from the *Britannia*'s bulletin, after calling at Tristan da Cunha, the impact – no matter how brief – was momentous on the simple daily routine of these lonely outposts:

'The Duke of Edinburgh ... accompanied by the Chief, boarded one of the longboats and at the Chief's invitation took the helm and he sailed the longboat ashore. On the beach he was greeted with the cheers of the fishermen while the womenfolk of the island added theirs from the cliff top. Behind the beach stood the canning factory for the island's main industry – crawfish – which His Royal Highness inspected on the way to the settlement. An amusing spectacle was the transferring of the instruments of the Royal Marines band by the ox-wagons from the beach. After climbing a cliff-side track Prince Philip arrived at a beautifully decorated archway of welcome, where he was greeted by Dr and Mrs Gooch, Mr Stapleford, the agricultural adviser, and his wife, and Mr Harding, the schoolmaster, and his wife. Donkeys, usually a familiar feature of the island, were absent, having been driven to the other side of the island lest they should eat the arch of welcome.'

The Prince was conducted by the Chief and the Administrator to a succession of thatched cottages where groups of women, dressed in their best clothes, were carding and spinning. 'It was in one of these cottages that Prince Philip received a special welcome from Martha Repetto, the head woman of Tristan ... he was shown an exhibition of the crafts of the island. These included ... knitted clothing, models of boats and marbles made from the eyes of dried bluefish. There should have been six of them, but the Chief's cat had swallowed two of them the night before.'

Prince Philip responds to the excitement and arduousness of tours, and it makes no difference whether he is received by crowds or few people; the zeal remains the same. They present the opportunity to see new faces and to mix with people from a wide spectrum of life. There is also the insatiable desire to explore new places and to savour fresh adventures. Typical had been the day he flew into Darwin from New Guinea during the previous November. Despite the exhausting heat, he entered wholeheartedly into a schedule of sight-seeing and hand-shaking. Crammed into the limited time, there was the pre-arranged tour of the Darwin wharves and Philip's appearance at a children's rally, as well as the unanticipated calls at a hospital and a trade union meeting before the Prince was driven over sixty-five miles of scorched bushland to the uranium mine at Rum Jungle. (Someone noted: 'The route was lined with the rare North Australian orchid – beer bottles – sign of the consistent thirst of the occupants.')

Returning to Darwin, Prince Philip could take only the briefest relaxation before attending a reception at Government House, where someone unexpectedly proposed a crocodile hunt. The nocturnal adventure won Philip's spontaneous approval: it would be ideal escapism from the official routine. Lightning and heavy rain in the torrid night failed to dissipate the Prince's enthusiasm, and as the party crossed the harbour, fierce waves broke over the open boat and completed the soaking. Graphic stories of the cunning and strength of crocodiles served as a diversion. George Haritos, the guide, explained how the tail of a big crocodile could send even a buffalo sprawling, and he warned Philip not to assume that because a crocodile was shot it was necessarily dead; without warning it could suddenly transform into a squirming killer.

Midnight was approaching as they penetrated the sandbanks and mangrove swamps – haunt of the crocodile, an eerie domain in the darkness and more sinister still as the boat's spotlight pierced the labyrinth of tangled vegetation. As the light pierced the nooks and crannies of the mud-banks, Haritos told Philip how to distinguish between a crocodile and a log. 'The eyes will look like burning cigarettes,' he said. The shot, he added, must be precisely to the brain, aiming between the eyes and a little below the centre, or shooting at an eye from the side. The crocodiles, it seems, were not rife that night; some while elapsed before anyone noticed the tell-tale eyes. Prince Philip took swift aim and despatched a six-foot reptile with a solitary shot. In time the skin, now tanned, arrived at Buckingham Palace to appear as handbags for the royal ladies.

To the disappointment of Prince Philip's entourage, the tour received only modest coverage in the British press. Not until early in 1957, when *Britannia* was journeying homewards from Gambia, did reports suddenly reach any magnitude. What amazed and troubled the Prince was the mendacity underlying their vexatious content. In London mischievous and baseless rumours purported that between the Queen and her young husband there was a rift. Elizabeth, they insinuated, bitterly resented the months Prince Philip had devoted to the tour. One could interpret the innuendo in various ways. The tour had coincided with a period of acute crisis. This was the aftermath of the Suez adventure when the Queen would doubtless have welcomed Prince Philip's advice; for although the Prince has no official status in the constitution, one would be naïve to imagine that the Queen did not discuss such matters with her Consort. That was irritating enough, but what was even more pernicious was the snide inference that the tour had been organized as a deliberate separation for a while; that the strain imposed on Philip in adjusting himself to the role of Consort had invaded his private life. Nothing could have been more alien to fact, and the reports were either a contemptible attempt to denigrate the Prince or revealed ignorance and crass stupidity. It should be obvious that because of the unavoidable complexities, royal tours – and certainly one of world proportion – are prepared many months in advance. Ignoring this, certain foreign newspapers (notably in Germany) irresponsibly pandered to fictitious hearsay – falsehoods that were repeated in the *Baltimore Sun*. As yet the British press had remained silent, but the Press Association now communicated with Buckingham Palace seeking confirmation or denial, and Sir Michael Adeane, the Queen's Private Secretary, announced : 'It is quite untrue that there is a rift between the Queen and the Duke of Edinburgh.' His words had the effect of unleashing on Britain the fabrications which so embittered the Prince.

At the Guildhall luncheon which traditionally concludes a royal tour, Prince Philip sarcastically explained that the journey had been completed 'against every expectation, to the day of our original estimate – perhaps unfortunately as it turned out'. (Some newspapers had implied a lack of enthusiasm to leave *Britannia* and fly home.) To be away from home as a sailor had 'meant nothing at all', but now it had more significance, he explained, returning to the long separation from the Queen and their children. 'I believe,' said Prince Philip, 'there are some things for which it is worth while making some personal sacrifices, and I believe that the British Commonwealth is one of those things and I, for one, am prepared to sacrifice a good deal if, by doing so, I can advance its well-being by even a small degree. This Commonwealth came into existence because people made sacrifices and offered their services to it ... if we don't make sacrifices for it we ... will have lost something of much greater value than just a grand conception.'

Temporarily the false allegations made Philip even more suspicious of the press. For some time, certainly in the early years of his marriage, the Prince's relationship had been strained. In an apt description of the situation, a Buckingham Palace secretary once said: 'Sometimes things would start fizzing. It was rather as if someone had opened a champagne bottle at the wrong temperature – with the result that someone else got the cork in his eye.' At times Prince Philip tended to develop a phobia of the press – more so the photographers – becoming hypersensitive over tactless intrusion in his private capacity. Typical was the day at Cowes when cameramen unreasonably came too close as he sailed his yacht. With his son Prince Charles, Prince Philip scrambled into a motor-boat and dashed off to deliver a torrent of abuse.

His feud with the press lasted for some years. When in Rio de Janeiro in 1962 he described the *Daily Express* as a 'bloody awful newspaper', the public wrongly assumed that Beaverbrook Newspapers, and not the press generally, was the main target of his invective. Reflecting on the Beaverbrook hostility towards Lord Mountbatten and the Prince, it was a pardonable error. Prince Philip indubitably directed his hate in that quarter – first in private, it is said, when his position was not consolidated, and in public later – but it was not an isolated instance; he was scathingly contemptuous of most purveyors of news and views. Despite the façade of toughness, Prince Philip seemed to be more vulnerable to criticism than was supposed. Maybe, of course, he was vehemently expressing himself against injustice. Speaking to American journalists at a luncheon in London in November 1962, he astonished them by his manifest repugnance for the British press. Accusing the *Daily Express* of being 'far too savage' in its vituperation (he was obviously still smarting from the criticism over royal expenditure from the *Sunday Express* and not the morning newspaper), he then censoriously judged the *Daily Mirror* to be 'not quite respectable'. But even that eminent organ of public opinion, *The Times*, did not escape criticism; he censured it as 'far too stodgy'. To widespread surprise, *The Guardian* received the royal accolade for being – in the Prince's view – the finest (and certainly his favourite) newspaper in Britain.

But these were the days of adjustment. Perhaps Prince Philip was not quite so sure of himself and less hardened to criticism. Before leaving his Palace duties, his private secretary, Michael Parker, wisely suggested to 'Dear Pippo' that he should create a highly efficient public relations organization to inject some cordiality into his dealings with the press. Prince Philip acted in due course, profitably to himself. But for some while the truce would remain somewhat fragile. The incidents demonstrating the friction would become legendary. To mention a few: the time when photographers were doused with water at the Chelsea Flower Show; the visit to see the apes at Gibraltar and the caustic remark – 'Which are the apes and which are the reporters?'; and the occasion when he swore at photographers at a polo match.

Against this the press has invariably snatched the chance to be captious, especially when he has honestly expressed what was paramount in his mind. Philip rejoins that criticism is a salient function of any free country. Doubtless his chief objective is to jerk the people from the malaise of inertia, or focus on some provocative point. He once argued, for instance, when addressing an audience of scientists: 'Progress is indiscriminating. Progress gives us better medical science, but it also gives us better bombs. How do you relate computers to compassion?' At a British air line meeting, he warned: 'British safety standards are lower than those of several other countries.' Unfortunately his comments in recent years have been less challenging and less inclined to evoke controversy. Probably the reason lurks in his introduction to a volume of his speeches: 'I try to say something which I hope may be interesting or at least constructive. To do this and at the same time avoid giving offence can sometimes be a ticklish business. I have come to the conclusion that when in doubt it is better to play safe – people would prefer to be bored than offended.'

7

A Contrast in Consorts

Some years ago, while his portrait was being painted in oils, Prince Philip examined the easel's mechanism, then described to the artist how the action could be improved to raise and lower the canvas. It was just another instance illustrating the Mountbatten passion and flair for technical achievement. Undoubtedly there is a pronounced streak of ingenuity in Prince Philip's mental make-up, and the desire to learn precisely how anything functions (and, if possible, enhance its performance) has been a lifelong characteristic. Even before his marriage, that same questioning mind was probing the potential status and functions of a consort in readiness for the time he became the husband of the Queen. Perhaps his ego was sharply deflated when he realized that the British constitution shuns the Queen's Consort completely.

'Constitutionally I don't exist,' sums up the position of the sixth consort of a queen regnant in British history. Circumstances had varied for each of his predecessors and could provide Prince Philip with neither precedent nor guidance as to privilege. The first consort had been Lord Guildford Dudley, husband of Lady Jane Grey. But as she reigned for a mere nine days, there was no time to assert himself before Consort and Queen were lamentably committed to the Tower of London. When Queen Mary I – 'Bloody Mary' who consigned Protestants to the flames – married King Philip of Spain, she ensured that the power of the Crown stayed scrupulously within her own control. It was rather different in the case of William of Orange. Politics and religion crept into the issue. For Protestant reasons, as William III he was invited by the Whigs to share the throne of Mary II, his Stuart wife. The Consort of their successor,

Queen Anne, would be Prince George of Denmark who, apart
from his duties as Lord High Admiral, would remain a royal
nonentity right to his death. Indeed, Queen Victoria, a century
and a half later, would unflatteringly dub him 'stupid old
George of Denmark'.

Coming to more recent times, Prince Philip, delving among
the Royal Archives at Windsor, resorted to reading about the
life of Queen Victoria's consort, his great-great-grandfather. For
the guidance and instruction of successors and posterity, he had
written: 'The position of prince consort requires that the
husband shall entirely sink his own individual existence in that
of his wife; that he should aim at no power by himself or for
himself; should shun all attention, assume no separate responsibility before the public, but make his position entirely a part
of hers, fill up every gap which as a woman she would naturally
leave in the exercise of her regal functions.'

The punctilious Albert might have regarded this as the ideal
formula for future consorts but it certainly did not apply to himself. 'Albert helps me with the blotting paper when I sign,' revealed Queen Victoria. But he also did much more. The Prime
Minister, Lord Melbourne, actually induced the Queen to communicate all foreign dispatches (something she later denied to
the heir apparent) to Albert. Indeed, the intellectual Prince,
who was better informed than many of the Queen's Cabinet
Ministers (it was claimed that in Britain's dealings with foreign
countries he 'got the government out of innumerable scrapes')
acquired such power that he began to fashion the monarchy
into what has been described as 'an indispensable occasional
department of State' – a plan ended by his death. But in the
final phase of his life he largely influenced the pattern of
monarchy as it is seen today. In 1840 he informed his father:
'Victoria allows me to take much part in foreign affairs, and
I think I have already done some good. I always commit my
views to paper, and then communicate them to Lord Melbourne. He seldom answers me, but I have often the satisfaction
of seeing him act entirely in accordance with what I have said.'
Despite his dictum to 'sink individual existence in that of the
Queen', in reality the reverse was the case; Prince Albert

wielded effective power from behind the throne. Few would have disputed this. Maybe tactlessly but truthfully King Louis Philippe of France, on visiting Windsor in 1844, told his hostess: 'Le Prince Albert c'est pour moi le Roi.' Instead of taking umbrage Queen Victoria later commented on her guest: 'How lively, how sagacious!'

Comparisons can be odious but it is enlightening to compare Prince Philip and his predecessor. In studying Prince Albert's life, Philip has made no attempt to imitate him, but although in the main their paths diverge, at least they do meet at certain points. Both Princes were of foreign birth: Albert was of the little German Duchy of Saxe-Coburg (which covered an area of about the size of Staffordshire) and Philip was a scion of the Royal House of Greece. Rightly or wrongly, because of their alien origin both were treated with suspicion by the British on marrying into the royal line. Prince Philip has finally won acceptance but Prince Albert never did completely. Yet to Prince Albert the dislike was mutual. An intellectual, he scorned much of the British way of life and, to express their resentment, the people – more so the nobility – were hostile to his naturalization as a Briton. Only the most prejudiced, however, would deny that his contribution to the monarchy was gargantuan. Certainly throughout the last decade of his life, his was the guiding hand that led Victoria. Happily in his final years he gained some of the prestige and respect that was due to him. Death deprived him of greater honour and, as Lytton Strachey pointed out, took from the State a man 'grown in the service of the nation, virtuous, intelligent and with the unmistakable experience of a whole lifetime of government'.

Prince Philip scored over his illustrious forebear by being admitted to the British peerage. So profound was the insular attitude towards Victoria's husband that both she and Melbourne considered it unwise to grant him an English title. Ironically, although he would reign jointly with Queen Victoria – in practice if not in theory – Albert (unlike Prince Philip) would never be allowed to take a seat in the House of Lords. Indeed, Prince Albert had to wait patiently for seventeen years before the Queen dared grant him the style and title of Prince Consort.

Plaintively he wrote to his brother: 'This ought to have been done ... at our wedding.' But the title had no intrinsic value and Albert lay dead four years later. With a tinge of sarcasm, *The Times* commented that 'the new title guaranteed homage to its bearer on the banks of the Spree and the Danube but made no difference in his position anywhere else'. Perhaps Prince Philip entertained a similar view. The appointment would be solely a matter for the Queen, but so far Philip himself has expressed no wish to be created Prince Consort. More significant, perhaps, was that in 1957 – a century after Prince Albert received his empty title – the Queen declared that her husband 'shall henceforth be known as His Royal Highness The Prince Philip, Duke of Edinburgh'. As in the case of Victoria's husband, Prince Philip received the Royal Warrant giving him precedence immediately after the Queen, thus placing him before his son and heir to the throne, the Prince of Wales.

In character and temperament Prince Philip has little, if anything, in common with his ancestor. The over-conscientious, rather self-righteous, profoundly religious and humourless Albert was the antithesis of the highly energetic, extrovert, witty and sometimes testy Philip. But like the Prince Consort, Philip has a keen, analytical and orderly mind.

The comparisons are interesting in other ways. Love of horsemanship took Prince Philip to the polo field. Prince Albert preferred prowess in the fox hunt, a royal pursuit which maybe contributed more than anything to win some regard from the English aristocracy. Albert was a fine marksman with a gun, but so too is Philip, although he bears no comparison with his great-great-grandfather in sartorial splendour. When he went shooting, the Prince Consort was magnificent in a black velvet jacket and long scarlet boots. To Queen Victoria he was 'very picturesque', but the British gentry, according to Lytton Strachey, thought the Consort looked 'more like some foreign tenor'. Here one senses royal incongruity. Albert, despite his introspection, favoured some flamboyancy in dress but Philip, who is extrovert in temperament, chooses restrained clothes and invariably dispenses with a hat (to the chagrin and despair of manufacturers).

In industrial matters both Prince Philip and his ancestor are on common ground. Philip accepted the honorary position of president of the British Association for the Advancement of Science. His connection with science was intended to give prestige and nothing more, but Prince Philip had other ideas. Still in command of *Magpie*, he worked on his speech – 'The British Contribution to Science and Technology in the Past Hundred Years' – during his last weeks at sea. It was a comprehensive speech, denuded of platitudes, but as Prince Philip has since remarked: 'I am not notably reticent about talking about things of which I know nothing.'

A vast audience gathered to hear him speak in the Assembly Hall of Edinburgh University and many more watched on closed circuit television. Maybe most of the people anticipated the speech with curiosity but never expected enlightenment. 'Your kind invitation to me to undertake the office of your President for the ensuing year,' he began, 'could not but startle me ... The high position which science occupies ... contrasted strongly in my mind with the consciousness of my own insignificance in this respect.'

Smiling, Philip remarked that this was a quotation from a speech by Prince Albert on a similar occasion in Aberdeen in 1859. That was his first surprise. Then came the jolt, exposing at the same time the Mountbatten insight into technical matters. Extolling the contribution of British scientists in the mid-nineteenth century for almost an hour, he reproved British industry for tending to stagnate and live on past successes. He warned: 'The rate at which scientific knowledge is being applied in many industries is too small and too slow. Our physical resources have dwindled, but the intellectual capacity of our scientists and engineers is as great as ever, and it is upon their ingenuity that our future prosperity largely depends ...' Scientific knowledge could either 'obliterate life itself' or rid the world of fear, hunger and drudgery. 'It is clearly our duty as citizens to see that science is used for the benefit of mankind. For what use is science if man does not survive.'

Remarks of that nature were not expected from someone so close to the throne; but the storm of applause echoed in the press the following day. Overnight Philip had grown in intellectual stature in British eyes. Over the years, science and technology for the betterment of society would be a recurring theme. At the opening of the Chesterfield College of Technology, for example, he stressed:

'There is no finality in any branch of human endeavour. If anyone tells you that there is not a better way of doing something, he is either a supernatural being or a supernatural clot. If you don't believe me I suggest you look around a bit more in your daily life and I guarantee there isn't a single man-invented gadget that couldn't do with a bit of improvement and ... every intelligent designer knows perfectly well he could and would do better next time.'

In his own era, Prince Albert, whose acute shyness gave a false façade of aloofness and arrogance, had felt impelled to awaken the nation to potentialities. The culmination of his enthusiasm for science and manufacture reached its peak in the Great Exhibition of 1851 – a magnificent monument to his aspirations for an industrialized Britain and the hope that new techniques would create a better society. But for his determination, this ambitious venture would never have matured. Yet it was accomplished only after great struggle, for he protested: 'The opponents work with might and main to throw all the old women into panic, and drive myself crazy.'

Prince Philip has broken down xenophobic barriers partly because of his essentially British upbringing. There is a story on record relating how, during one of his many factory tours, an admirer asked: 'Well, sir, and how do you like it in this country?' 'I've been here all my life,' explained Philip. 'How do you?' Fiction or fact, this anecdote illustrates that Britain has exerted more influence on the Prince than any other country. In his formative years, he was educated on English lines, not with the object of becoming the Queen's Consort but solely to gain a permanent commission in the Royal Navy. Virtually the reverse obtained in the case of Prince Albert. Marriage to Queen Victoria was pre-arranged by their mutual grandmother, the Dowager Duchess of Coburg, not long after Albert's birth. On her death in 1831 their uncle, Leopold I of the Belgians, assumed the role of royal marriage-maker. That Prince Albert would one day be the Queen's Consort was established by the death of William IV's second daughter during childhood in 1821. (Princess Victoria was next in line to the throne and became heiress presumptive when only two.) Albert was therefore specifically trained to be a sovereign's helpmeet right from infancy; and when the union was effected in 1840 it was merely the fulfilment of years of grooming. Tragically the British public declined to accept him as anything but an alien. Philip, in contrast, had certain attributes: a British education, ultimate service in the Royal Navy, and an uncle with an adventurous career in the Second World War. Moreover, Prince Philip is self-contained, and assured in his own judgments and decisions, whereas Prince Albert's alienation was accentuated partly by his recruitment as confidant of Baron Stockmar from his Uncle Leopold. Born in Coburg, Stockmar exerted tremendous influence over Prince Albert and therefore over the Queen herself. Indeed, Stockmar's personality intruded into Palace life in a manner which Prince Philip would never tolerate.

Philip, as has been explained, has not escaped criticism or detractors but he has never suffered such calumny as was directed by the press towards the Consort. Even Queen Victoria's uncles treated him with suspicion. At one stage rumours were even circulated that he had been arrested for high treason. To Stockmar he complained: 'You will scarcely credit that my being committed to the Tower was all over the country – nay even that the Queen had been arrested. People surrounded the Tower in thousands to see us brought to it.'

If anything, the most graphic contrast between the Prince Consort and Prince Philip was in the education that each planned for the respective heirs apparent. Albert's grandiose plan – probably the most comprehensive for a royal heir in British history – was disastrous. The future Edward VII learned more from 'the horse-copers, dog-fanciers and rat-catchers who formed the best undergraduate society' than from the combined efforts of the Consort and Stockmar who strove to evolve a philosopher-king. Prince Philip was revolutionary but patently practical, preparing a blueprint which, for the first time in the thousand-year-old history of the monarchy, guaranteed a liberal education for the heir apparent. It was a bold experiment, designed to equip the future King Charles III for monarchical duties in the late twentieth or twenty-first century. To W. E. Gladstone, Stockmar was merely a mischievous old prig, but to Queen Victoria and the Prince Consort he was a moulder of royal perfection. To the boy-Prince, who was left in isolation, he was a source of misery (albeit unwittingly). Lord Melbourne endeavoured to ease the strain, warning the Queen to be 'more solicitous about education. It might be believed to do much, but it is not as much as is expected from it'. Foolishly Victoria ignored him and Albert planned his son's future with meticulous care, from the appointment of Mrs Lily, the nurse, to the selection of a scientific tutor. Said Stockmar pompously: 'The nursery gives me more trouble than the government of a kingdom would do.' Starved of the companionship of boys of similar age Prince Albert Edward languished daily in the loneliness of the schoolroom. Not until his twentieth year did he decide himself what he should read. ('Every book came before me as a task.')

There would be no tutorial tyranny for Prince Charles. Indeed, the centuries-old practice of teaching the heir apparent strictly within the purlieus of the Palace ended abruptly. Prince Philip knew that in these times of rapid social upheaval, the monarchy could not remain apathetic to change. Down the years the British monarchy had survived chiefly because, with or without coercion, it had met the challenge of change. Prince Philip's part in preparing Prince Charles for kingship in a restless democratic age has much significance; on the success or failure of the experiment could well depend the destiny of the British monarchy.

The Queen and Prince Philip could not escape the latter-day Stockmars, the Left-wing intellectuals who knew best how to educate other people's sons. Since Prince Charles had been born in an age of the common man, they argued, it was imperative – in compliance with true democratic principles – that he should pass through State schools to acquire knowledge of the working classes. Thus the homogeneous world of his future subjects would open up like an immense kaleidoscope before the future Charles III. It is essential in modern kingship for a sovereign to communicate with ordinary men. This does not mean, however, that he has to conduct himself like them. Neither would rational people expect it, for Prince Charles is no ordinary citizen and never could be due to accident of birth. The Queen and Prince Philip rightly ignored the ranting voices in more liberal circles.

It is now clear that Prince Philip was the architect of his son's educational future. After an introductory period at Hill House, an exclusive day school in Hans Place, Knightsbridge, Prince Charles attended Cheam and then tackled the rigours of Gordonstoun. Two terms at Timbertop, the unconventional offshoot of Geelong Church of England Grammar School on the timbered heights of Mount Buller in Victoria, dispelled the last traces of an embarrassing shyness which would have been painful in kingship. Three years as an ordinary student at Trinity College, Cambridge, were interrupted by the Welsh interlude – two terms spent at the University College of Wales – prior to his investiture as Prince of Wales.

Like his father, Prince Charles emerged the type of person that (in Kurt Hahn's words) Gordonstoun strives to create:

'He will have a trained heart and a trained nervous system which will stand him in good stead in fever, exposure, and shock; he will have acquired spring and powers of acceleration; he will have built up stamina and know how to tap his hidden resources. He may enjoy the well-being which goes with a willing body. He will have trained his tenacity and patience, his initiative and fore-thought, the power of observation and his power of care. He will have developed steadfastness and he will be able to say "No" to the whim of the moment. He will have stimulated and nourished healthy interests until they become lively and deep, and perhaps develop into a passion. He will have discovered his strength.'

This had been the educational formula for the Queen's Consort; Prince Philip chose it for his son.

Prince Philip has instilled high ideals not merely into his own offspring but also into British Commonwealth youth. Some years ago the government of the day offered to give him access to confidential state documents, like the Queen. He declined, however, realizing that by accepting he would deny himself freedom of expression. Apart from this, whereas Prince Albert's interests centred more on the dispatch boxes, Prince Philip's penchant is inclined towards causes. In consequence, perhaps his finest monument as yet is his Award Scheme, his imaginative venture for youth which materialized from a few pencil notes on his desk in 1954. His aim was to encourage young people to make the best use of their leisure – and 'to help them make the transition from child to adult'. Here one suspects the Gordonstoun influence. The Scheme was not to be competitive. Instead, participants would 'discover new interests ... measure themselves against all reasonable standards ... (and) testing and strengthening their own character'. Entrants must qualify in some form of public service, become accomplished in a leisure-time occupation, and attain certain standards in physical fitness.

Since its inception in the autumn of 1956, the Scheme has grown into an integral part of society, not only in Britain but in the Commonwealth, too. Prince Philip's ideas are those used in the upbringing of his own children. He contends that young people should be exposed 'to as many new experiences as possible. Anything which has not been done before has an element of adventure – even if it is only spending a night in a tent for the first time. Children go through a phase of being prepared to learn to experiment. Later on there is a sense of embarrassment at being a beginner.' He is not opposed to exposing young people to risk provided it is minimized by proper training. ('The only real danger is ignorance. Proper training removes most of the hazards, in what, to the uninitiated, look like dangerous activities.') In two decades more than one million young people would participate in the Scheme and roughly half would receive Awards. In encouraging adolescence to make the best use of its leisure, Prince Philip is attempting to improve people's minds and counter crime and vandalism. Here again one detects the influence of Hahn who, sensitive to the sickness of modern society, tried to regenerate it through the development of individual character. First he infected his pupils with his ideals then they – his disciples – influenced others; in short, a human chain reaction. Hahn's credo for Philip and his fellow students was to afford not only opportunities for self-discovery but to learn to cope with danger as well as triumph; to be self-effacing in a common cause; to train the imagination; to make games important but not predominant; and to foster periods of silence and loneliness. Hahn was convinced that 'no intellectual life worthy of the name can be expected to develop if there is no opportunity and no desire to be alone'. Prince Philip recognized the wisdom inherent in his mentor's remarks and would write: 'I had the opportunity of walking over the hills of Scotland and finding moments of solitude and reflection invaluable to a young man who is trying to keep a balanced out-look in ... modern life'.

Prince Albert did not share Prince Philip's enthusiasm to assist youth, but each, in his own way, considered it his duty to affect changes concerning the monarchy. It is now known that Queen Victoria owed much to her Consort's patient guid-ance and political sagacity. It was not appreciated at the time but he gave stability to the monarchy and it was only endangered through the Queen's folly by going into prolonged purdah after his death. He tussled with the sprawling monster of financial waste which had undermined Palace affairs over the years. Servants and trades people had even benefited from household laxity. While poring over the Palace housekeeping accounts he was appalled to discover that because an order had not been cancelled, two thousand coloured candles had been delivered daily since a ball held eight years previously. For the domestic staff candles were a coveted perquisite, for once they had been lit and extinguished, they were discarded. At the conclusion of a function, these 'Palace ends', as they were christened, were snatched from sconces by the footmen who secured high prices for them in the shops.

Albert pruned Palace extravagance to the extent that he saved £200,000 from the royal housekeeping – sufficient to purchase Osborne House on the Isle of Wight, Victoria's most cherished home. His patronage he gave to the Royal Navy and the Army – largely instigating the inception of the military training centre at Aldershot. London's first working-class flats were the outcome of his enterprise, and his skill in foreign affairs avoided Britain's involvement in the American Civil War.

The erosion of royal powers since the Victorian era has circumscribed Prince Philip's ability to imitate his predecessor in matters of State assuming that he had the desire to do so. The sovereign still retains the right to be consulted, to encourage and to warn, but to what extent, if any, Prince Philip has exercised influence over the Queen will not be known for years to come, if ever. Meanwhile, like the Prince Consort, he has made an impression on household economies. At Buckingham Palace, soon after the Queen's accession, Prince Philip personally visited all members of the staff and discussed with them their duties in detail; where efficiency could be intensified, action was taken. Time-wasting infuriates him. To reduce the time when changing dress, he designed a wardrobe which automatically ejects a particular suit or uniform at the press of a button. At Clarence House an innovation was a dictagraph installation linking all the offices by direct line. An enlarged version was introduced to Buckingham Palace in June 1953, together with a number of amplifying sets. Like Lord Mountbatten, he is a push-button enthusiast, and favours electronically-operated doors, windows and blinds. A push-button television set was even installed in the Queen's bedroom so that programmes could be changed from the bed. Considerable use is made of tape-recorders and he communicates with his secretaries and family by means of walkie-talkie. In Britain he was a pioneer in equipping his cars with radio-telephone so that he could speak to the Queen or staff when he was driving. His time and motion studies have increased the tempo of life throughout the royal household. At Buckingham Palace, Philip found certain long-standing practices much too tiresome; for instance, on returning

to the Palace late at night, the Queen could not simply ring a bell
or ask on the house phone for light refreshment; such requests
had to be dealt with by at least four people. Breakfast, too, by
Philip's standard, was much too tedious. The Palace kitchens
are remote from the dining-room, and so he started to cook
his meals in the bedroom on an electric frying-pan – a decision
which is reminiscent of Rowlandson's cartoon portraying Queen
Charlotte frying sprats at an open fire. Queen Elizabeth may
have admired her Consort's enterprise but disliked the lingering odours. Meals were served as before. She favours, however, his invention of a swivel-mounted kettle for making early
morning tea. To widen the range of diet at Buckingham Palace,
Prince Philip dispatched the royal chef to Paris to extend his
knowledge of Continental cooking. Paradoxically, he eventually
complained about the absence of simple English fare.

In streamlining the royal estates at Windsor and Sandringham, Prince Philip has introduced working methods to effect
financial stability. The Windsor gardens form a vital facet of
the household's economy. To reduce the cost in the royal homes
– especially in the kitchens at Buckingham Palace – they maintain a regular flow of flowers and vegetables. To meet the
demands of staff and guests, twenty-four acres are devoted solely
to vegetables and a further eight acres are allotted to fruit.
About two acres are set aside for flowers, and a slightly lesser
area is under glass. At Sandringham, whatever is grown is sold,
whether it is birds, beef, timber or fruit. Under Prince Philip's
supervision, Sandringham's 20,000 acres have witnessed a
variety of experiments; for instance, mushroom growing, carrot-
washing machines, and the preparation of frozen peas. Each
year black currants are grown over fifty acres for a commercial
firm.

Of the monarchy itself, as far as is conceivably possible,
Philip has dove-tailed it into modern requirements. To a
question at a luncheon of the Foreign Press Association, the
Prince replied:

'What you are implying is that we are old-fashioned. Well,
that may easily be true. I do not know. One of the things about

the monarchy and its place, and one of its great weaknesses, is that it has to be all things to all people and, of course, it cannot do this when it comes to being all things to people who are traditionalists and all things to people who are iconoclasts. We therefore find ourselves in a position of compromise and we might be kicked by both sides. The only thing is that if you are very cunning you get as far away from the extremists as you possibly can because they kick harder. I entirely agree that we are old-fashioned. It is an old-fashioned institution. The interesting thing about the monarchy is that it not a monopoly of old people.'

Realistic in his approach to monarchical change, he is profoundly conscious of the intricacies entailed. In a debate on the monarchy at Oxford University, he argued that one of the 'peculiarities of this home of democracy and free speech is that there is a convention that members of the Royal Family are expected to refrain from practising free speech on matters loosely termed political. The most assiduous guardians of this convention are members of the House of Commons. I presume this is in case any of us can be quite so profoundly stupid as to say something with which Members might disagree.'

To Canadian separatists in the sixties, he bluntly remarked: 'I think it is a misconception to imagine that the monarchy exists in the interests of the monarch. It doesn't. It exists in the interest of the people.' With even greater candour, he added: 'I think the important thing about it is that if at any stage people feel it has no further part to play, then for goodness sake let's end the thing on amicable terms without having a row about it.'

If the politicians suspect that royalty are liable to err on the side of stupidity, Prince Philip has also ruefully assessed that the 'art world thinks of me as an uncultured polo-playing clot'. The belief clings with limpet doggedness that he is barren of artistic appreciation. This is not so; he is both a discerning patron and, like his predecessor, the Prince Consort, he is a competent amateur artist himself. Rather than stalk deer at Balmoral, Prince Albert's practice was to sit in a hide in the heather, whiling away the time with a sketchbook until the quarry came within range. Grappling without instruction with the technique of oil painting, Prince Philip diffidently showed some canvases to Annigoni when the Italian master painted the Queen's portrait at Buckingham Palace. In his critical appraisal, Annigoni detected a force which was rather uncommon in a novice. 'I don't claim any exceptional interest or knowledge or ability' is Prince Philip's own assessment of himself, and he would write to Feliks Topolski: 'The people concerned in our collections view me with horror and suspicion.' Whether this is exaggeration or not, many young painters are grateful for Prince Philip's patronage. The first painting he ever commissioned was a miniature portrait of the Queen, as Princess Elizabeth, by Stella Marks. Sir James Mann, the royal art expert, advised Philip on the choice of artist and borrowed paintings from Mrs Marks to show to an unnamed friend. Today this water colour on ivory is Philip's most cherished painting.

As a naval lieutenant on shore leave in Sydney an exhibition by William Dobell, the Australian artist, left an indelible impression on the Prince. He could not afford to give patronage in those days, but some years later he commissioned two works from Dobell, who was eventually knighted. The Apap brothers in Malta, who first attracted him with their small caricature statues, benefited likewise. He commissioned eight statues – the figures of Sir Winston Churchill, Lord Avon, Earl Mountbatten, Field-Marshal Montgomery, and the Archbishop of Canterbury among them. But William Apap was a serious painter and Philip commissioned a portrait of his daughter, Princess Anne, and from brother Vincent, a sculptor, a bronze head of Prince Charles.

What might present itself as a casual visit to an exhibition invariably proves profitable to someone. For instance, at a Scottish Academy show, red labels appeared on eighteen pictures after Prince Philip had scrutinized them. Viewing works by members of the Royal Society of Painters in Water Colours, he bought four etchings by a young artist, Alan Carr Linford, for the private rooms of *Britannia* and later commissioned twenty-four water colours of Windsor and his sisters' German homes and a Darmstadt scene. A further sixteen coloured drawings of London's river originally adorned the staircase at Clarence House but were then transferred to Windsor. Perhaps somewhat odd considering his love for the sea, he rid a gallery at Buckingham Palace of its portraits of admirals interspersed with battle scenes to make way for a 100-foot portrayal of the Queen's coronation which he commissioned Topolski to paint. His inclinations towards the paintings of Edward Seago prompted him to invite the Norfolk artist to accompany him to the Antarctic to paint whatever he pleased.

His own paintings are rather scattered. Some have been donated and others hang at Wood Farm, which the Royal Family now use at week-ends to obviate the high cost of using the great mansion. At Windsor his paintings that are not stored decorate Prince Charles's apartments and guest rooms. Prince Philip favours still life, landscapes (particularly of Norfolk scenes) and places he has recorded on his travels.

At times the Prince is himself the subject of paintings. Edward Halliday alone has painted five portraits. At one sitting the artist believed Philip was making notes for a speech when he in fact was drawing Halliday. It was Halliday who awakened Philip's zeal for industrial design. While painting the Gordonstoun portrait, Halliday mentioned casually that Gordon Russell, the designer, was organizing an exhibition, 'Design at Work'. In face of critics, Philip crusaded with Russell to ally beauty and function and championed the inception of the Design Centre in London to encourage the finest in industrial design. The Duke of Edinburgh's Prize for Elegant Design is today a coveted annual award.

'Industrial design, or art in industry [he said outspokenly to the Convocation of the Royal College of Art], is really a misnomer. The artist or designer may work in industry, but the stuff he designs ends up in the home, in the street, in the office and in the workshop. I'm sure that people like seeing and living with nice things. I believe that the critical faculty is not automatically switched off on leaving an art gallery.

After all, most people take their eyes with them to work, just as they do to the National Gallery or the bathroom ... You're lucky if you own a picture painted by an RA, but most people have got to live with furniture, domestic objects, cars, shops, pubs, and everything else that surrounds us in our daily lives. It's inevitable that we should see more advertisements than old masters.'

This keenness for appropriate design extends to the awards associated with himself. He is averse to the traditional silver cup, expecting a trophy to be in keeping with whatever it identifies. When, for instance, the show business philanthropists, the Grand Order of Water Rats, suggested a greyhound trophy, Prince Philip jocularly proposed a silver lamp-post but finally designed a silver dog collar. Many awards are made in the Prince's name and due to his undoubted enthusiasm in that sphere, some relate to sports. He is president, patron or honorary member of some two hundred sporting bodies. Discounting all other factors, Prince Philip has earned British respect for his prowess as an athlete and sportsman. To his detriment, Prince Albert had neither much inclination nor skill in sports. Fate, however, seemed to decree that sport should be a cardinal factor in Philip's life. Indeed, he made his first public speech at a sporting event. During August 1934 an advertisement in the local newspaper at Cromer announced that 'the Greatest Gymkhana ever held in Norfolk' was to be staged at the Norfolk Riding School on behalf of the 'crab-boat disaster fund'. The centre of the event was HRH Prince Philip of Greece, who would present the prizes. Readers were puzzled. Who was Prince Philip? Fortuitously on the eve of the gymkhana, the national press disclosed the engagement of Prince George, Duke of Kent, to Princess Marina of Greece. The news stimulated even greater curiosity in the mysterious Philip who, to the surprise of the crowd at Cabell Park, happened to be a smiling rather dishevelled thirteen-year-old schoolboy. Philip's appearance had been planned by Commander Oliver Locker-Sampson, a onetime pupil at Cheam.

Prince Philip was a spectator that day but, as people would

learn, the role of observer is not compatible with his temperament. 'I don't like watching,' he once revealed. 'I have plenty of years ahead to go on watching sports. At the moment I want to play them.' His attitude is summed up in the words: 'People taking exercise feel happier and better for it.' Sport, moreover, is an antidote to the stresses and pressures of modern life. He has consistently focused attention on industrial man's need for recreational and sports facilities, and it is a theme to which he has frequently returned. He himself could not have withstood the rigorous routine of public service but for intense personal physical fitness. The Palace gymnasium, once almost as silent as a tomb, has been in perpetual demand over the last twenty-five years. Apart from the normal paraphernalia, he has introduced rowing machines and other devices, including a mechanized horse to perfect his polo shots.

There are few sports which Prince Philip has not experienced, but his versatility and accomplishments are too detailed to recount. One illustration must suffice to illustrate his almost fanatical enthusiasm for sport – a passion which ranks down the centuries with other royal athleticism when a prince was expected 'to ride cumlie, to run faire at the tilt or ring, to plaie at all weapons, to shote faire in bow, or surelie in gon'. During 1958 Prince Philip's Windsor Park team had qualified to meet Brewhurst in the final for the Royal Windsor Cup, the main polo event of Ascot week. Bad weather, however, caused a postponement which coincided with a detailed schedule of engagements with the Queen in Northumberland and Scotland. An added setback was an injury to one of the more skilful players, Colonel Gerard Leigh. The prospect of two less experienced substitutes was unthinkable. Philip promised that somehow he would play. It was a predicament which he found exhilarating. After reading the second lesson at a church service at 12.10 p.m., he accompanied the Queen to the market place on Holy Island for a tree planting ceremony, to be followed by a tour of the island by Land Rover. But the Queen travelled alone while Philip discreetly walked to the lifeboat station to board the royal barge from *Britannia*. At Seahouses, eight miles down the coast, a car hurried him over the twenty-four miles to the RAF station at Acklington. There he joined a Heron of the Queen's Flight, ate a picnic lunch and at 3.35 the aircraft landed at a Berkshire airfield. From there the Prince drove in his Lagonda to Smith's Lawn in fifteen minutes. The match started at 4.15 and Philip's team won.

In the meantime, *Britannia*, with the Queen on board, had left the vicinity of Holy Island and headed north for the Firth of Forth. That evening Prince Philip returned to the Heron at White Waltham and flew to Turnhouse near Edinburgh, rejoining the Queen by motor-boat.

Nowadays Prince Philip's sporting pursuits are less strenuous. He is at his happiest perhaps in the half-light of a chilly dawn, setting out to shoot wild fowl, and seeking anonymity in a 'boat-sucking, ooze-reeking, sea-filled creek' in the Fenlands, or shooting wild boar on his sisters' German estates. (He had practised markmanship at similar hours at Gordonstoun, firing at rock pigeons with a 6-millimetre pistol.) On occasions he is vehemently criticized for his readiness to use a gun and at the same time advocate conservation. A typical stricture was voiced in the House of Commons: in Standing Committee while debating a Bill for the protection of deer, someone drew attention to 'the Duke of Edinburgh, who goes in for this loathsome kind of sport and even brings his child [Prince Charles] up to do it.'

To the charge of hypocrisy, Prince Philip replied to critics when, speaking at the diamond jubilee dinner of the Wildfowlers' Association, he said:

'Pesticides, insecticides, poison and pollution have destroyed more life than man has ever taken, and by affecting the capacity to breed and by destructive interference in the food chain, whole populations of species are being exterminated. What man as a hunter has failed to do in millions of years, man as a business man and scientist is achieving in a couple of generations, and with every general approval. We seem to exist with a rather strange morality in this country. Everything which is pleasant must of necessity be sinful, and everything that is done for money – that is, professionally – cannot possibly be enjoyable.'

To Prince Philip shooting and conservation are not contradictions. He has learnt that many amateur naturalists 'go into it [conservation] through shooting, stalking or fishing'.

As co-author of *Wildlife Crisis*, a book describing the world's threatened animals and natural areas, the Prince revealed that his enthusiasm for watching and photographing birds was fired during the frequently gale-ridden voyage in *Britannia* in 1956. *Birds from Britannia*, which is also amply illustrated by the Prince's own photographs, is an account of the islands and land masses visited by Prince Philip on that and another voyage three years later. Both books are a stark warning that it is 'only a matter of a short time of innocent birdwatching and photography before the question of survival of species begins to dawn on the mind'.

About the time Prince Philip was returning from the Antarctic, a party of naturalists assembled in the Palacio, an ancient hunting lodge in that faunistic paradise – the Marismas of the Guadalquivir in south-east Spain. Here on one of the great estates, the Coto Donana, the late Sir Julian Huxley, Guy Mountfort, and Max Nicholson deplored the non-existence of a well-financed movement organized to tackle the conservation crisis, such as the development plans then menacing the survival of the Spanish wilderness. With the aid of Prince Philip and other eminent naturalists and conservationists, the World Wildlife Fund was born in 1961 to raise money for conservation projects throughout the world. As president of the British National Appeal, in the sixties he twice visited the Galapagos Islands and took part in the film *The Enchanted Isles* that dealt with this volcanic archipelago and was shown on television all over the world. For *Now or Never*, another conservation film, decrying vanishing wild life, Prince Philip, as international trustee, visited Lake Rudolf in northern Kenya where wild life abounds. The Abbruzzi National Park in Italy and the Marchanen reserve in Austria, together with his involvement in the natural reserve problems of Australia, are irrefutable evidence of his principle that 'the fundamental lesson [is to guarantee] that if you want any game animals the following year you have to ensure a proper breeding stock and a suitable habitat'.

Both in speeches and in writing, he has campaigned for conservation. For instance, while at the Empire Games in Perth, Australia, he induced the authorities to abandon plans for a holiday village at Two People Bay to avoid endangering – and in one case exterminating – rare species of birds.

It is not sycophancy to suggest that such concessions are made as much as anything out of deference to the Prince. The esteem has grown over the years. In November 1947, on his marriage to Princess Elizabeth, his life as a naval officer changed spectacularly overnight. He was twenty-six, and inevitably faced a responsibility that was daunting. For twenty-five years now he has served as the Consort of Queen Elizabeth II, an exacting task which, to some degree, has made him subordinate his personality. Constitutionally, as already stressed, he does not exist. Yet from this nebulous and ironical situation he has emerged a significant personality on the world scene. Curiously this public attention is not necessarily of his own choice; indeed there have been times when he has fiercely shunned publicity, as expressed in bursts of temper towards an intrusive press. When he first came under the glare of publicity, he quickly arrested as an individualist who had neither the desire nor the intention to conform to the traditional image associated with royalty. Not for him the fetters and the stifling routine which was once imposed on the Royal Family. Instead, mainly due to upbringing, he has retained the common touch without losing dignity, and like no other British prince before him speaks the language of his fellow citizens. What he says might be unpredictable and to some even unpalatable. 'I sometimes think,' he pungently told American correspondents in London, 'that it is a pity the peace of the world is left to politicians who are a quarrelsome lot.' And to the President of the Republic of Paraguay, he remarked: 'It is a pleasant change to be in a country which is not ruled by its people.'

This modern prince has never been scared to kick open the door of controversy. It can be argued that, considering that the State offers him no place in the constitution, he is privileged to do so. Nor is he afraid to lace his comments with humour and the odd dose of irreverence for the absurd. Hence, over the years, such news headlines as 'Philip in Tinned Fruit Uproar' and 'Duke Angers Drainage Men'. A keen intelligence and an incisive mind spur him to curb the ponderous talk of others. At least his trenchant remarks, whether one agrees with him or not, cause people to think, and it is likely that even his severest critics will concede that he fulfils a difficult task superlatively well. He is extremely secure today as the First Gentleman of the Realm and is doubtless conscious of his influence, but he has not allowed it to become intoxicating. He is acutely aware of the neutral tightrope which royalty must walk, a fact which must irritate when – as Prince Bernhard of the Netherlands once wrote – 'some ideas of either or both of us, of which no one has been able to convince us that they are not feasible or wrong, are not put into practice or tried out or even considered, because the executive power lies in other hands'. Is this why the princely gadfly feels compelled occasionally to sting? Whether or not one agrees with his beliefs, at least there is refreshing clarity and candour as opposed to the duplicity and make-believe so rife today.

Regrettably far too many people have ignored his uncompromising principles: the desire, for example, for better human relations and the obvious need for the integration and efficiency of scientific and industrial spheres. Years ago warning against the possibility that Britain might become the poor relation of the Commonwealth, he stressed: 'No amount of talk will prevent this happening. Hard work with imagination is our only chance.'

Cynics have scoffingly described him as a 'latter-day John the Baptist' and 'monarchy's answer to the modern world'. Prince Philip's own account of himself is that he is 'self-employed', trying to react to what people expect. 'In addition, I feel that I may have a position. Whatever influence I have I want to use for the benefit of the country. Needless to say, there are some ways that I'm invited not to.' But his appeal is wide. A public opinion poll revealed this 'one-man royal ginger group' as Britain's most popular candidate for President or Dictator. One also hazards the guess that the majority of his fellow citizens would endorse the remark of Sir Cullum Welch, a former Lord Mayor of London, who once said: 'You have opened up to us, sir, a quite new vision of the potentialities latent in the position of a royal consort in the twentieth century. You do not please the half-hearted, the defeatists, the players for safety. But you delight and thrill the eager, the energetic and the brave.'

Select Bibliography

Lee, Arthur S. Gould, *The Royal House of Greece*, 1948
HRH Prince Philip, Duke of Edinburgh, *Selected Speeches*, 1957
HRH Prince Philip, Duke of Edinburgh, *Prince Philip Speaks*, 1960
HRH Prince Philip, Duke of Edinburgh, *Birds from Britannia*, 1962
HRH Prince Philip, Duke of Edinburgh, and Fisher, James, *Wildlife Crisis*, 1970
Sutherland, Douglas, and Purdy, Anthony, *The Royal Homes and Gardens*, 1966
Tisdall, E. E. P., *Royal Destiny*, 1955
Cathcart, Helen, *The Royal Bedside Book*, 1969
Boothroyd, Basil, *Philip*, 1971
HM ex-Queen Alexandra of Yugoslavia, *Prince Philip, A Family Portrait*, 1959
HRH Prince Andrew of Greece, *Towards Disaster*, 1930
Channon, Sir Henry, *'Chips' (Diaries)*, 1967
HRH Prince Christopher of Greece, *Memoirs*, 1938
Cookridge, E. H., *From Battenberg to Mountbatten*, 1966
Hatch, Alden, *The Mountbattens*, 1966
Bocca, Geoffrey, *Elizabeth and Philip*, 1953
Dean, John, *HRH Prince Philip, A Portrait by his Valet*, 1954
Kerr, Mark, *Prince Louis, Admiral of the Fleet*, 1934
Connell, Brian, *Manifest Destiny*, 1953
Hilton, James, *The Duke of Edinburgh*, 1956
Liversidge, Douglas, *Queen Elizabeth II: The British Monarchy Today*, 1974
Liversidge, Douglas, *Prince Charles: Monarch in the Making*, 1975

Index